WORKBOOK PLUS
TCAP PRACTICE
GRADE 4

 HOUGHTON MIFFLIN HARCOURT

Illustrations

Elizabeth Allen: 11, 22, 34, 97; **Burgandy Beam:** 16, 98, 141; **Catherine Bennett:** 120; **Linda Howard Bittner:** 8, 64; **James Buckley:** 20, 132; **Donna Catanese:** 142; **Randy Chewning:** 91; **Lisa Chiba:** 95; **Rondi Collette:** 51, 55, 66, 73, 77, 87, 103, 105, 116; **Alexandra Delange:** 28; **Eldon Doty:** 82; **Marion Eldridge:** 158; **Larry Frederick:** 83; **Patti Goodnow:** 14; **Patti Green:** 49, 152; **Reggie Holladay:** 99, 101; **Tim Jones:** 115; **Victor Kennedy:** 2; **Robert Masheris:** 151; **Tom McKee:** 93, 127, 153; **Michele Noiset:** 63, 79, 118; **Bill Petersen:** 126; **Phyllis Pollema-Cahill:** 157; **Bart Rivers:** 26, 32; **Tim Robinson:** 60; **Slug Signorino:** 68, **Gregg Valley:** 7, 107, 129; **Bill Whitney:** 109; **Toby Williams:** 64, 122, 146

ISBN-13: 978-0-547-32975-8
ISBN-10: 0-547-32975-X

9 10 0928 14 13 12
4500367188

Table of Contents • Workbook Plus

Part 2
Writing, Listening, Speaking, and Viewing

Table of Contents • TCAP Practice

Daily Practice Tests

WORKBOOK PLUS

Name _____

Writing Good Sentences

Complete sentence	Sacajawea helped Lewis and Clark explore western America.
Incomplete sentence	In 1805.
Sentences combined	Sacajawea helped Lewis and Clark explore western America in 1805.
Two incomplete sentences	Explorers Meriwether Lewis and William Clark. Traveled 8,000 miles in 28 months.
Sentences combined	Explorers Meriwether Lewis and William Clark traveled 8,000 miles in 28 months.

Writing Complete Sentences 1–5. Rewrite this paragraph from an essay. Fix the incomplete sentences by combining them or adding each to a complete sentence.

Revising

Sacajawea helped Lewis and Clark in many ways. When they explored the American West. She could translate Native American languages for the explorers. Because she was the daughter of a Shoshone chief. Sacajawea had grown up in the territory Lewis and Clark were exploring. Along the Missouri River. Sacajawea helped the explorers build a friendship with a Shoshone chief. The chief became very helpful. When he found out that Sacajawea was his long-lost little sister! The generous Shoshone. Provided horses, supplies, and information needed by the explorers for crossing the Rocky Mountains.

_____
_____
_____
_____
_____
_____
_____
_____
_____

(continued)

Grade 4: Unit 1 The Sentence *(Use with pupil book pages 34–35.)*
Skill: Students will write complete sentences by combining complete and incomplete sentences.

WORKBOOK PLUS TCAP PRACTICE 3

Name _____

Writing Good Sentences (continued from page 3)

| Unclear meaning | All nine planets orbit the sun. Following an oval path. They also rotate on their own axes. |
| Complete sentences | All nine planets orbit the sun following an oval path. They also rotate on their own axes. |

Writing Complete Sentences 6–12. Rewrite this paragraph from a science book. Fix each incomplete sentence by adding it to a complete sentence or to another incomplete sentence.

Revising

Earth is a planet. Rather than a star. Planets differ from stars because they cannot produce their own light and heat. Earth receives the energy it needs. From the sun. We can see other planets shining in the night sky. Because they also reflect the sun's light. Rotation, the motion of spinning on an axis, is a feature of the planets. Earth completes one rotation. Every twenty-four hours. Planets also differ from the stars because they travel, or revolve, around the sun. Earth makes one complete trip around the sun. In one year. Planets that are farther from the sun than Earth must travel a greater distance. Over a greater period of time to make a complete revolution. It takes Saturn nearly thirty Earth years. To circle the sun just once!

_____

_____

_____

_____

_____

_____

_____

_____

_____

Grade 4: Unit 1 The Sentence *(Use with pupil book pages 34–35.)*
Skill: Students will write complete sentences by combining complete and incomplete sentences.

Name _____

2 Statements and Questions

Statements	Questions
We are having stew for dinner.	Are we having stew for dinner?
We do have all the ingredients.	Do we have all the ingredients?

A Write the correct end mark for each sentence. Write *S* for statement or *Q* for question.

1. Did you ever help to make a pot of stew_____ _____

2. I like to make stew with my uncle_____ _____

3. We put carrots, beans, meat, and potatoes in a pot_____ _____

4. Did I remember to tell you that we add water_____ _____

5. Then we let the stew cook slowly for several hours_____ _____

6. We always keep a lid on the pot_____ _____

B 7–15. This letter has three missing capital letters and six incorrect or missing end marks. Use proofreading marks to correct the letter.

Example: Is minced meat pie a dessert �?

Proofreading

Proofreading Marks	
¶	Indent
∧	Add
୭	Delete
≡	Capital letter
/	Small letter

Dana,

You'll never guess what Uncle Otis cooked for us last night it's called minced meat pie. have you ever tried it. It looks like a regular fruit pie until you slice it Inside the pie is a dark brown filling of apples, raisins, brown sugar, cinnamon, and chopped beef? It tastes okay if you drink milk with it what will Uncle Otis think of next.

Yours truly,

Alex

(continued)

Grade 4: Unit 1 The Sentence *(Use with pupil book pages 36–37.)*
Skill: Students will identify and punctuate statements and questions.

WORKBOOK PLUS
TCAP PRACTICE 5

© Houghton Mifflin Harcourt Publishing Company

2 Statements and Questions (continued from page 5)

Challenge

Match the riddles with their correct answers. Add the correct end marks.

QUESTIONS	STATEMENTS
1. What is a frightened clock called _____	A sponge is _____
2. Why did the girl put her dollar in a sandwich _____	It's called an alarm clock _____
3. What is full of holes and still holds water _____	It was her lunch money _____
4. Why did the gardener wash her hands _____	It gets all steamed up _____
5. How does a carrot feel when it gets angry _____	A bookworm does _____
6. What animal lives in a library _____	She had a green thumb _____
7. Where did the car go swimming _____	It swam in a car pool _____

Now make up three riddles of your own, using questions and statements.

QUESTIONS   STATEMENTS

_____   _____

_____   _____

_____   _____

Writing Application: An Interview _____

   Suppose that you are hiring a cook to work for you. Write three questions you might ask the cook. Write three statements that describe your favorite foods for the cook.

Grade 4: Unit 1   The Sentence   *(Use with pupil book pages 36–37.)*
Skill: Students will punctuate and will write statements and questions.

3 Commands and Exclamations

Commands	Exclamations
Don't forget your manners.	How important manners are!
Please listen carefully.	What a great teacher you are!

A Write the correct end mark for each sentence. Label each sentence *command* or *exclamation*.

1. How important manners are ____   _____

2. Always thank your friends after they help you ____   _____

3. Use the word *please* when asking for something ____   _____

4. Hold the door for the person behind you ____   _____

5. Never talk when someone else is talking ____   _____

6. How annoying that is ____   _____

B 7–15. Anna's poster has three missing capital letters and six incorrect or missing end marks. Use proofreading marks to correct the poster.

Example: How annoying bad telephone manners are**!**

Proofreading

Proofreading Marks

¶ Indent
∧ Add
⌐ Delete
≡ Capital letter
/ Small letter

Telephone Manners

• Be polite and friendly.

• say your name clearly

• Listening carefully is a must

• how rude it is to chew gum

on the telephone.

• speak slowly

• Do not shout into the phone!

• Hang up the receiver quietly

(continued)

Grade 4: Unit 1   The Sentence   *(Use with pupil book pages 38–39.)*
Skill: Students will identify and will punctuate commands and exclamations.

WORKBOOK PLUS
TCAP PRACTICE

7

Name _____

3 Commands and Exclamations (continued from page 7)

Challenge

Unscramble the letters in the robot to make words. Match these words to the correct sentence parts to make commands and exclamations.

ROBOT UNRAVEL

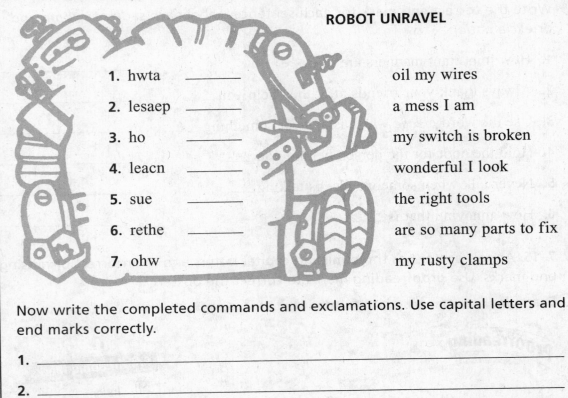

1. hwta _____
2. lesaep _____
3. ho _____
4. leacn _____
5. sue _____
6. rethe _____
7. ohw _____

oil my wires

a mess I am

my switch is broken

wonderful I look

the right tools

are so many parts to fix

my rusty clamps

Now write the completed commands and exclamations. Use capital letters and end marks correctly.

1. _____
2. _____
3. _____
4. _____
5. _____
6. _____
7. _____

Writing Application: A Journal

Suppose that you are teaching your new pet to behave. Write at least three commands and two exclamations that tell how you would train your pet. Be sure to use capital letters and end marks correctly.

Grade 4: Unit 1   The Sentence   *(Use with pupil book pages 38–39.)*
Skill: Students will write commands and exclamations correctly.

4 Subjects and Predicates

Complete Subjects	Complete Predicates
Many inventors	lived in Philadelphia, Pennsylvania.
Some inventors	became famous.

Draw a line to divide the complete subject and the complete predicate of each sentence. Write *CS* above the complete subject and *CP* above the complete predicate.

1. Thomas Edison invented the light bulb.

2. Some inventions are practical.

3. Other inventions are fun.

4. The first bicycle was built over one hundred years ago.

5. A man from England built the first modern bicycle.

6. Television became popular in the United States.

7. This invention is over eighty years old.

8. People bought their first frozen foods in 1925.

9. Levi Strauss made the first denim pants in 1847.

10. Many people call them jeans.

11. Gold miners were Levi's best customers.

12. The telephone is not a new invention.

13. Many inventions change over the years.

14. A cellular telephone is one example of this change.

15. The computer is another example.

16. Computers have become smaller and more powerful.

17. Scientists are not the only inventors.

18. Many ordinary people invent.

19. We hear of new inventions all the time.

20. New products help many people.

(continued)

Grade 4: Unit 1 The Sentence *(Use with pupil book pages 40–41.)*
Skill: Students will identify complete subjects and complete predicates.

WORKBOOK PLUS
TCAP PRACTICE

9

Name _____

4 Subjects and Predicates (continued from page 9)

Challenge

Look at the lists of inventions for the future. Write a sentence that describes what each invention will do. Underline the complete subject and circle the complete predicate of each sentence.

Outdoor Inventions	Indoor Inventions
1. Way Finder	4. Dish Swisher
2. Power Center	5. Floor Crawler
3. Star Searcher	6. Sweeper Beeper

1. _____

2. _____

3. _____

4. _____

5. _____

6. _____

Draw a picture that shows one or two of the inventions above.

Writing Application: An Advertisement

Suppose that you are an inventor. Write an advertisement for one of your inventions. Write the name of your invention. Then write five sentences that describe what it looks like and what it does. Draw a line between the complete subject and the complete predicate of each sentence.

Grade 4: Unit 1   The Sentence   *(Use with pupil book pages 40–41.)*
Skill: Students will identify complete subjects and complete predicates.

5 Simple Subjects

Subjects	Predicates
My favorite **holiday**	comes every February 14.
It	is Valentine's Day.

Underline the complete subject of each sentence. Write the simple subject.

1. Mrs. Marcus told our class about Valentine's Day.   _____

2. Valentine's Day has an interesting history.   _____

3. Many stories about the first Valentine's Day exist.   _____

4. One story links this day to an old Roman festival.   _____

5. Romans held this festival on February 15.   _____

6. The oldest known Valentine's Day card dates from 1415.   _____

7. Heart–shaped cards are exchanged in modern times.   _____

8. They can be funny or serious.   _____

9. Many people show their feelings with presents.   _____

10. Some shy people send unsigned cards.   _____

11. Ties in fancy boxes are gifts for some valentines.   _____

12. Pretty flowers are also popular on Valentine's Day.   _____

13. Boxes of candy fill the stores around Valentine's Day.   _____

14. Valentine's Day may be celebrated for many more years.   _____

(continued)

Grade 4: Unit 1   The Sentence (*Use with pupil book pages 42–43.*)
    Skill: Students will identify simple subjects and complete subjects.

**WORKBOOK PLUS
TCAP PRACTICE**   **11**

Name _____

5 Simple Subjects (continued from page 11)

Challenge

Underline the simple subjects in the sentences below. Use them to complete the puzzle.

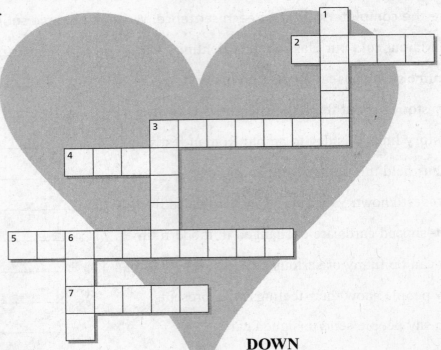

ACROSS

2. Red roses are a sign of love.

3. My favorite holiday is February 14.

4. Rome celebrated one of the first Valentine's Days.

5. Valentines are fun to give and to receive.

7. Most valentine cards are pink, red, and white.

DOWN

1. Bobby sent Lucy a valentine.

3. My heart belongs to you!

6. White lace with pink ribbon looks pretty on a card.

Writing Application: A Personal Narrative

Think about your favorite holiday. Write five sentences that tell how you celebrate this holiday with your family or friends. Underline the simple subject of each sentence.

Grade 4: Unit 1 The Sentence *(Use with pupil book pages 42–43.)*
Skill: Students will identify simple subjects.

Name _____

6 Simple Predicates

Subjects	Predicates
Everybody	**dreams** during sleep.
Some people	**forget** their dreams.

Underline the complete predicate of each sentence. Write the simple predicate.

1. Scientists study people's dreams. _____

2. Signals come from the brain during sleep. _____

3. Scientists attach wires to a person's head. _____

4. A special machine measures light sleep and heavy sleep. _____

5. Light sleep lasts for about two hours. _____

6. Dreams occur during certain stages of sleep. _____

7. Some people dream many dreams in one night. _____

8. Dreams happen in about two hours of a night's sleep. _____

9. Some sleepers awake in the middle of a dream. _____

10. Many people remember their dreams. _____

11. Dreams seem real to the dreamer. _____

12. Some dreams appear in color. _____

13. Dreams are important to many scientists. _____

14. They learn about the brain from people's dreams. _____

(continued)

Grade 4: Unit 1   The Sentence   *(Use with pupil book pages 44–45.)*
Skill: Students will identify simple predicates and complete predicates.

WORKBOOK PLUS
TCAP PRACTICE   13

Name _____

6 Simple Predicates (continued from page 13)

Challenge

The children below have dreams for the future. Write a sentence about each child, following the directions below.

1. Katya loves animals. Write a sentence about Katya, using the simple predicate *dreams.* _____
   _____

2. Wesley loves airplanes. Write a sentence about Wesley, using the simple predicate *hopes.* _____
   _____

3. Tokie loves working with clay. Write a sentence about Tokie, using the simple predicate *wants.* _____
   _____

4. Rico loves growing flowers. Write a sentence about Rico, using the simple predicate *wishes.* _____
   _____

Now write a sentence about a dream that you have for your future. Underline the simple predicate.

_____

Writing Application: A Journal

Suppose that you have come from another country to live in the United States. What are your dreams for a new life? Write at least five sentences that describe your feelings on your first day in the United States. Underline the simple predicate of each sentence.

Grade 4: Unit 1   The Sentence   (*Use with pupil book pages 44–45.*)
Skill: Students will write and will identify simple predicates.

Name _____

7 Correcting Run-on Sentences

Incorrect	Storms bring rain and snow they can also bring hail.
Correct	Storms bring rain and snow. They can also bring hail.

A Write each run-on sentence correctly. Write *correct* if the sentence is not a run-on.

1. Some storms cause problems the effects depend on where you live.

   _____

   _____

2. Strong winds blow during a storm thunder booms sometimes.

   _____

3. Winds above the Earth's surface can reach more than 75 miles per hour.

   _____

4. A rainstorm can be very dangerous to crops and farm animals.

   _____

B 5–10. Use proofreading marks to correct the six run-on sentences in this report.
Example: Some storms bring plenty of rain. heavy rain can damage land.

Proofreading

BULLETIN!

Proofreading Marks

¶ Indent
∧ Add
⌿ Delete
≡ Capital letter
/ Small letter

You can keep yourself safe in a tornado follow some

important rules. Listen to a radio when the weather is bad go

to a safe place when you hear a warning. Stay away from

windows go to an inside room or hallway. Basements are safe places getting under

a heavy table or the stairs gives you extra protection. Bathrooms are good you

can even get into an empty bathtub. If you are outside, stay away from power

lines. Go to a ditch or other low ground. Plan ahead what you will do have a

tornado drill every year.

(continued)

Grade 4: Unit 1   The Sentence   *(Use with pupil book pages 46–47.)*
Skill: Students will identify and correct run-on sentences.

WORKBOOK PLUS
TCAP PRACTICE

15

Name _____

7 Correcting Run-on Sentences (continued from page 15)

Challenge

Correct each run-on sentence by adding periods and capital letters. Then write the first letter of each sentence in the blanks.

1. Strong winds and fast air currents can form a jet stream it is like a huge tube of air.   _____ _____

2. Centers of storms are called eyes eyes are usually calm.   _____ _____

3. Some storms are made of ice ice storms can hurt people.   _____ _____

4. Dangerous ice storms can destroy trees these storms coat the trees with ice.   _____ _____

5. One ice storm can cause problems on the roads usually roads get slippery.   _____ _____

6. Lightning flashes during a storm thunder rumbles later.   _____ _____

7. Observing the weather is a scientist's job deciding the path of a storm is important.   _____ _____

Now unscramble the letters to write a common expression about winter weather.

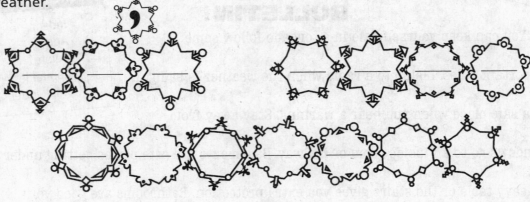

Writing Application: A Weather Report

DESCRIBING

Write a weather report for a TV news program. Write five sentences that describe a serious storm and what the storm does to your area. Be careful not to write any run-on sentences.

Grade 4: Unit 1   The Sentence   (Use with pupil book pages 46–47.)
Skill: Students will identify and will correct run-on sentences.

Name _____

Writing Good Sentences

Run-on sentence	On the Fourth of July, Americans celebrate their independence they observe the birthday of their nation.
Corrected sentence	On the Fourth of July, Americans celebrate their independence, **and** they observe the birthday of their nation.

Combining Sentences 1–6. Rewrite the following letter describing Sam's favorite holiday. Correct each run-on sentence by adding a comma and the word *and*.

Revising

Dear Tony,

The Fourth of July is my favorite holiday our town always has such a wonderful party! The celebration begins with a parade. Marching bands come from all over the state they play lively music. A barbecue follows the parade everyone eats hot dogs and watermelon. Kids compete in sack races many people play softball. After sunset, bright colors explode across the sky the day ends with an awesome display of fireworks. I wish you could be here to join in the fun!

Sincerely,

Sam

_____

_____

_____

_____

_____

_____

_____

_____

_____

_____

(continued)

Grade 4: Unit 1 The Sentence *(Use with pupil book pages 48–49.)*
  Skill: Students will correct run-on sentences by adding a comma and the word *and*.

Name _____

Writing Good Sentences (continued from page 17)

Short, choppy sentences	Many coin tricks look hard. They are actually easy to do.
Compound sentence	Many coin tricks look hard, **but** they are actually easy to do.

Combining Sentences 7–12. Rewrite the following paragraph from a book about magic tricks. Combine the underlined pairs of short sentences by adding a comma (,) and the word that is in parentheses.

Revising

Many people enjoy magic shows. Few people understand how tricks are done. (but) Most magicians practice their skills for hours. They perform tricks to entertain. (and) Much of their magic is based on illusion. One thing seems to be happening. Something different actually occurs. (but) A good magician can misdirect the attention of the audience. Spectators are led to focus on a magic wand or on one of the magician's hands. They do not notice the movement of the other hand. (and) Did the coin really disappear? Did the magician simply hide it in her palm? (or) People are curious about how tricks work. Magicians do not tell their secrets. (but)

_____
_____
_____
_____
_____
_____
_____
_____
_____

Grade 4: Unit 1 The Sentence (*Use with pupil book pages 48–49.*)
Skill: Students will combine short sentences by adding commas and connecting words to form compound sentences.

2 Common and Proper Nouns

> proper noun   common noun
> | |
> **Janet Guthrie** drives a race **car**.

A Write the nouns in each sentence. Be sure to write each proper noun correctly.

1. janet guthrie was born in iowa city, iowa.

_____

2. The young woman bought a special automobile.

_____

3. Her first race at watkins glen in new york lasted six hours.

_____

4. This bold driver entered the indianapolis 500.

_____

5. Her car was called the texaco star.

_____

B **6–16.** This part of a research report has eleven capitalization errors. Use proofreading marks to correct the report.

Example: In this contest, ms. guthrie finished near the top.

Proofreading Marks

¶ Indent
∧ Add
⟋ Delete
≡ Capital letter
/ Small letter

Proofreading

In 1977, janet guthrie became the first woman

driver to compete in the Indianapolis 500. That year

she also won an award, Top rookie, at the Daytona 500 race.

Because of her accomplishments, ms. guthrie was one of the first

women chosen to be in the women's sports hall of fame. Her

driving helmet and suit are in the smithsonian institution.

(continued)

Grade 4: Unit 2 Nouns *(Use with pupil book pages 66–67.)*
Skill: Students will identify common and proper nouns.

WORKBOOK PLUS
TCAP PRACTICE   **21**

2 Common and Proper Nouns (continued from page 21)

Challenge

Richmond County holds a road rally each year. The map below shows the race route and all the checkpoints where the drivers must stop. The map is incorrect because the proper nouns are not capitalized. Write each proper noun correctly on the lines below.

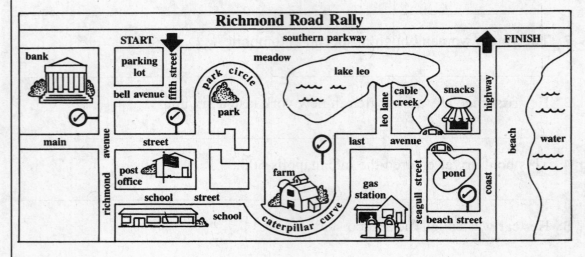

1. _____ 6. _____ 11. _____

2. _____ 7. _____ 12. _____

3. _____ 8. _____ 13. _____

4. _____ 9. _____ 14. _____

5. _____ 10. _____ 15. _____

Now, on the map above, draw the fastest route for your car. Be sure to stop at each checkpoint.

Writing Application: An Interview

Suppose that you have been asked to interview a sports champion. Write at least three questions that you will ask about the places where this person has competed and the people whom this champion admires. Then write the answers the person would give. Underline all the common nouns and circle all the proper nouns.

22 **WORKBOOK PLUS**
TCAP PRACTICE

Grade 4: Unit 2   Nouns *(Use with pupil book pages 66–67.)*
Skill: Students will identify and write common and proper nouns.

3 Singular and Plural Nouns

Singular	apple	day	class	box	lunch	brush
Plural	apples	days	classes	boxes	lunches	brushes

A Write the plural form of the noun in parentheses to complete each sentence.

1. Many _____ take part in the county fair. **(club)**

2. Last year our club won a lot of _____. **(award)**

3. We grew fifty perfect _____. **(peach)**

4. We took them to the fair in five _____. **(box)**

5. Two _____ thought that our fruit was the best. **(judge)**

6. Several cash _____ were given for the best quilts. **(prize)**

7. The winners made their quilts from _____ of cloth. **(patch)**

8. Our neighbor won a prize for the six largest _____. **(radish)**

9. Aunt Lou entered two _____ in the sewing contest. **(dress)**

B 10–14. Use proofreading marks to correct five plural nouns in this list of county fair expenses.

Example: 4 ~~ride~~ *rides* on the Giant Wheel $6.00

Proofreading

Proofreading Marks	
¶	Indent
∧	Add
⌐	Delete
≡	Capital letter
/	Small letter

• 8 game-booth ticket $8.00

• 2 tickets for the Cyclone Roller Coaster $3.00

• 2 cheese sandwich $2.50

• 3 helium balloon $3.00

• 5 glass of pink lemonade $3.00

• Basket of fresh peach for Granddad $5.50

TOTAL $25.00

(continued)

Grade 4: Unit 2 Nouns *(Use with pupil book pages 70–71.)*
Skill: Students will form plural nouns by adding -s and -es.

**WORKBOOK PLUS
TCAP PRACTICE**

25

Name _____

3 Singular and Plural Nouns (continued from page 25)

Challenge

Carver County is having a fair. There will be contests and games. Make three signs for the fair, using the plural form of each noun listed below. Decorate the signs with drawings or fancy lettering.

GARDENING CONTEST

cucumber	peach
radish	apple
box	berry

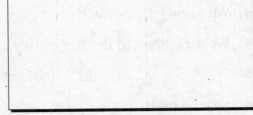

SEWING CONTEST

patch	blanket
quilt	shirt
dress	stitch

REFRESHMENT STAND

egg	glass
sandwich	plate
juice	salad
cheese	dish
lunch	snack

Writing Application: A Letter

EXPRESSING

Write a letter to the mayor about having a fair in your city or town. Write at least six sentences that tell how you would run the fair. Use the plural form of four nouns from the Word Box.

judge	lunch	circus	prize	dish	box

Grade 4: Unit 2   Nouns   (*Use with pupil book pages 70–71.*)
Skill: Students will form plural nouns by adding *-s* and *-es*.

4 Nouns Ending with y

Singular Nouns	Plural Nouns
one canary	many canaries
a play	some plays

Write the plural form of the noun in parentheses to complete each sentence.

1. _____ are an interesting way to learn. (Hobby)

2. Raising _____ is one way to learn about animals. (puppy)

3. Some people read _____ and try to solve them. (mystery)

4. Rabbit lovers might collect stuffed _____. (bunny)

5. Carl collects stamps from many different _____. (country)

6. He also has an interesting collection of _____. (key)

7. Jeremy collects anything to do with old _____. (buggy)

8. Lara buys _____ made out of glass or metal. (pony)

9. She also has two clay _____. (donkey)

10. Some people collect old _____ and piggy banks. (toy)

11. Aunt Grace has some beautiful painted _____. (tray)

12. On sunny _____ Ian looks for flowers to press. (day)

13. He has pressed eight kinds of _____. (daisy)

14. There are many _____ to have fun with hobbies. (way)

15. Kelsey collects post cards from all her friends' _____. (journey)

16. Some people even like to collect pits from _____. (cherry)

17. John takes pictures of lampposts in all the _____ he visits. (city)

18. The students made a collage from pictures of their _____. (family)

19. The prize for the display was five _____ for each student. (candy)

20. The students decided to have hobby day on all _____. (Friday)

(continued)

Grade 4: Unit 2 Nouns *(Use with pupil book pages 72–73.)*
Skill: Students will write the plural forms of nouns ending with y.

WORKBOOK PLUS
TCAP PRACTICE   27

Name _____

4 Nouns Ending with y *(continued from page 27)*

Challenge

Circle the plural nouns in the puzzle. Use the clues to help you.

CLUES:

1. They are hard to solve.
2. These places have many buildings.
3. These animals hang from trees.
4. They have soldiers in them.
5. These are the days before today.
6. They hop from place to place.
7. These animals can carry heavy loads.
8. People have them on special days.
9. Children play with them.
10. People act in them.
11. They were once caterpillars.
12. Boats sail on them.

```
B A N P O S I C K A
U M Y S T E R I E S
T O E B A V U T K O
T N S B U N N I E S
E K T O Y S D E F P
R E E R B A Y S M A
F Y R A C M O V S R
L S D O N K E Y S T
I L A R M I E S B I
E M Y A B E G U O E
S J S I D P L A Y S
```

keys   pennies

Writing Application: A Newspaper Article

Suppose that you are writing an article about hobbies for your school newspaper. Tell your readers about some interesting hobbies. Use the plural forms of five nouns from the Word Box.

| daisy | play | country | puppy | holiday | monkey |

Grade 4: Unit 2 Nouns *(Use with pupil book pages 72–73.)*
Skill: Students will write the plural forms of nouns ending with *y*.

Name _____

5 More Plural Nouns

Singular Nouns	Plural Nouns	Singular Nouns	Plural Nouns
this **woman**	some **women**	one **sheep**	eight **sheep**
each **foot**	both **feet**	a **moose**	both **moose**
a **mouse**	several **mice**	that **deer**	these **deer**

Write the plural form of the noun in parentheses to complete each sentence.

1. All the _____ honked as they flew by. **(goose)**

2. The farmer bought some _____ for his farm. **(ox)**

3. My yard is filled with _____. **(mouse)**

4. Look out the window at the flock of _____. **(sheep)**

5. Three _____ are in the play. **(woman)**

6. The dentist has to fill two holes in my _____. **(tooth)**

7. My _____ hurt after hiking for an hour. **(foot)**

8. At eight o'clock, the _____ go to sleep. **(child)**

9. There are two _____ in the woods. **(moose)**

10. Some _____ are crossing the road. **(deer)**

11. A few _____ refused the prize money. **(man)**

12. The child has lost two _____. **(tooth)**

13. All the _____ have left the pasture. **(sheep)**

14. Are four _____ sitting at the table? **(woman)**

15. How many _____ are between the floor and the loft? **(foot)**

16. Many _____ ran through the woods that day. **(deer)**

17. How are _____ like cattle? **(ox)**

18. It is fun to watch the _____ fly. **(goose)**

19. Will the _____ help in the barn? **(child)**

20. Five _____ had to haul the broken tractor. **(man)**

(continued)

Grade 4: Unit 2 Nouns *(Use with pupil book pages 74–75.)*
Skill: Students will write the plural forms of irregular nouns.

**WORKBOOK PLUS
TCAP PRACTICE** 29

Name _____

5 More Plural Nouns (continued from page 29)

Challenge

Below are ads for imaginary products. Fill in each blank with the plural form of a noun from the Word Box.

| tooth | sheep | man | deer | child | mouse | foot |

Zoom Sneakers make your _____ feel as light as air.

Zoom Sneakers make you run as fast as _____.

Dr. Flossa Lott cares about your _____.

She even teaches young _____ to brush!

Now use the plural forms of some of the words from the Word Box to create your own ad.

Writing Application: A Journal

Suppose that you have just visited the zoo. Write five sentences, describing what you saw at the zoo. Use the plural form of five nouns from the Word Box.

| deer | ox | sheep | child |
| woman | foot | man | moose |

Grade 4: Unit 2 Nouns *(Use with pupil book pages 74–75.)*
Skill: Students will write the plural forms of irregular nouns.

7 Plural Possessive Nouns

Plural Nouns	Plural Possessive Nouns
The nest belonging to the **mice** is small.	The **mice's** nest is small.
The singing of the **birds** is loud.	The **birds'** singing is loud.

A Write each sentence another way. Use the possessive form of each underlined plural noun.

1. We visited the farm owned by our <u>grandparents</u>.

   _____

2. The crowing of the <u>roosters</u> woke us up.

   _____

3. Then the shouts of some <u>children</u> rang out.

   _____

4. The cow that belonged to the <u>farmers</u> was missing.

   _____

B 5–8. The following poster for a science fair schedule has four incorrect plural possessive nouns. Use proofreading marks to correct the nouns.

Example: 8:00 A.M. How Dogs Become ∧Sheeps Guards *Sheep's*

Proofreading

Proofreading Marks	
¶	Indent
∧	Add
ℛ	Delete
≡	Capital letter
/	Small letter

Garfield School Science Fair

9:00 A.M.   Mooses Eyesight: Do They Need Glasses?

11:00 A.M.   Whales Brains Are Big, But Are Whales's Brains Best?

2:00 P.M.   Why Zebras's Stripes Are Like Fingerprints

(continued)

Grade 4: Unit 2   Nouns   *(Use with pupil book pages 78–79.)*
Skill: Students will form plural possessive nouns.

WORKBOOK PLUS
TCAP PRACTICE   33

Name _____

7 Plural Possessive Nouns (continued from page 33)

Challenge

You want to cross the Creature Town Zoo to meet your grandfather for lunch at the Feeding Time Cafe. Your map is missing the names of the landmarks along the way. Name each landmark by using a plural possessive noun. Write each name on the map. The first one has been done for you.

LANDMARKS

1. caves of bears
2. nests of birds
3. hives of bees
4. colonies of ants
5. burrows of rabbits
6. holes of moles
7. dens of foxes
8. lairs of lions
9. webs of spiders
10. lodges of beavers

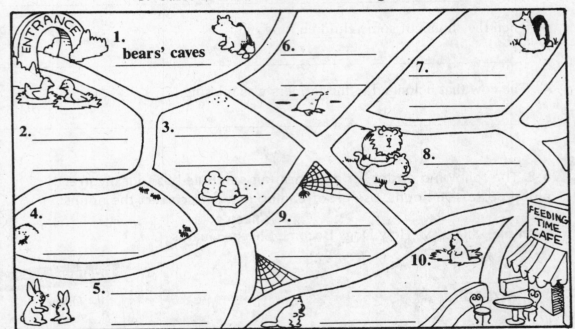

Now draw the path you will take from the entrance to the Feeding Time Cafe.

Writing Application: A Journal

 DESCRIBING

Think about a trip that you have taken. It might be a trip to a farm, a zoo, or a circus. Write at least five sentences about your trip. Describe the animals and the people you saw. Use a plural possessive noun in each sentence.

Grade 4: Unit 2 Nouns (Use with pupil book pages 78–79.)
Skill: Students will use plural possessive nouns correctly.

Name _____

3 Present, Past, and Future (continued from page 40)

Challenge

Make up your own mystery story, using the words in the columns below. For each sentence, choose a person from the first column, a clue from the second column, a place from the next column, and a time from the last column. Add your own verb and other words that you need. Be sure that each verb you use is in the correct tense. Use as many words from the lists below as you can.

PEOPLE	CLUES	PLACES	TIMES
Mr. Jones	wallet	to New York	yesterday
my teacher	secret papers	at home	now
Detective Silvio	locked door	in a desk at school	tomorrow
the "Ace"	hidden key	on the car	two weeks ago
my sister	package	in her office	soon
the dentist	envelope	at the police station	in a few years
Grandpa	footprints	on the kitchen table	today

Example: _My sister found a package on the kitchen table yesterday._

_____

_____

_____

_____

_____

_____

_____

Writing Application: A Review ——————— EXPRESSING

Think of a favorite mystery book or movie. Write a review of it. Use present tense verbs to tell what happens in the story. Use past tense verbs to tell what you thought of the story. Use future tense verbs to tell what others will think about this story.

Grade 4: Unit 3 Verbs (Use with pupil book pages 100–101.)
Skill: Student will write present, past, and future tense forms of verbs.

WORKBOOK PLUS
TCAP PRACTICE
41

Name _____

Writing with Verbs

Mixed tenses	Benjamin Franklin was a great statesman and inventor. He travels to France to get help for the American colonies during the Revolutionary War.
Same tense	Benjamin Franklin was a great statesman and inventor. He **traveled** to France to get help for the American colonies during the Revolutionary War.

Keeping Verbs in the Same Tense 1–8. Rewrite this part of an article about Benjamin Franklin so that every verb is in the same tense.

Revising

Benjamin Franklin was involved in many businesses in his life, but he is always reading and writing. He learns to read at an early age. He became an apprentice printer in 1718, when he reaches the age of twelve. At sixteen Franklin is in charge of his brother's newspaper.

Franklin's most famous work is *Poor Richard's Almanack,* a yearly calendar that includes wise sayings by "Poor Richard." These sayings encourage good habits such as honesty and hard work. Many colonists respect Benjamin Franklin and his writing.

_____

_____

_____

_____

_____

_____

_____

_____

_____

_____

(continued)

42 WORKBOOK PLUS
TCAP PRACTICE

Grade 4: Unit 3 Verbs *(Use with pupil book pages 102–103.)*
Skill: Students will rewrite paragraphs to make verbs the same tense.

Name _____

5 Spelling the Present Tense (continued from page 46)

Challenge

Suppose that you write reviews of plays for your school newspaper. You have seen the five new plays listed below. Write a short description of each play so that other students can decide which ones to see. In each description, use the verb in parentheses with a singular subject.

1. *Catch a Magic Star*

   (catch) _____

   _____

2. *The Wish*

   (wish) _____

   _____

3. *Try, Try Again*

   (try) _____

   _____

4. *The Case of the Buzzing Bee*

   (buzz) _____

   _____

5. *The Fix-It Kid*

   (fix) _____

   _____

Writing Application: Instructions

EXPLAINING

Suppose that you are the stage manager for the school play. It has six actors. The director has asked you to write notes that explain what each actor does on-stage. Use forms of some verbs from the Word Box.

watch	cross	relax	try	push	catch	hurry	buzz

Grade 4: Unit 3   Verbs   *(Use with pupil book pages 106–107.)*
Skill: Students will use present tense verbs with singular and plural subjects.

WORKBOOK PLUS
TCAP PRACTICE   47

6 Spelling the Past Tense

dust + -ed = dusted	bak**e** + -ed = baked	ch**op** + -ed = chopped	tr**y** + -ed = tried
stay + -ed = stayed	pil**e** + -ed = piled	b**eg** + -ed = begged	carr**y** + -ed = carried

A Write the past tense of the verb in parentheses to complete each sentence.

1. We _____ at our old summer cottage yesterday. (**arrive**)

2. We _____ our bags into the cottage. (**carry**)

3. First, we _____ all of the windows. (**open**)

4. Then Dad and I _____ the floors. (**mop**)

5. Mom _____ wax on the furniture. (**spray**)

6. I _____ the furniture with a dry cloth. (**rub**)

7. We _____ back the curtains. (**tie**)

B 8–15. This letter has eight misspelled past tense verb forms. Use proofreading marks to correct the past tense verbs.

divided
Example: We ~~divide~~ up the cleaning jobs.
       ∧

Proofreading Marks

¶	Indent
∧	Add
℘	Delete
≡	Capital letter
/	Small letter

Proofreading

Dear Jonas,

Last night, I dreammed about my cat Humbert. He diped his tail in a

bucket of soap suds. He moppd the kitchen floor. Then he hurryd to the yard.

He pourred water on the rose bushes. He chopped down a tree and carryed

it away on his back!

Then I woke up. I rememberied that I helped clean the kitchen yesterday.

I saw Humbert on my bedroom floor. He just smiled in his sleep.

Yours truly,

Althea

(continued)

Grade 4: Unit 3 Verbs *(Use with pupil book pages 108–109.)*
Skill: Students will form the past tense of regular verbs.

Name _____

6 Spelling the Past Tense (continued from page 48)

Challenge

This special robot does all kinds of kitchen jobs. Each night it prints out sentences describing the jobs it did that day. Write the robot's list for today. Use the past tense of a verb from the drawing in each sentence.

| bake | beat | chop | measure |
| boil | wash | stir | dry |

JOBS I DID TODAY

1. _____
2. _____
3. _____
4. _____
5. _____
6. _____
7. _____
8. _____

Writing Application: A Description

Suppose that you run a housecleaning service. Describe how you cleaned up someone's house or apartment. Use the past tense form of six of the verbs from the Word Box.

| pile | dust | mop | stack | carry | rub | push | dry |

Grade 4: Unit 3 Verbs (Use with pupil book pages 108–109.)
Skill: Students will form and will use the past tense of regular verbs.

WORKBOOK PLUS TCAP PRACTICE 49

7 The Past with Helping Verbs

Present	Past	Past with Helping Verbs
direct	directed	(has, have, had) directed
arrive	arrived	(has, have, had) arrived
drop	dropped	(has, have, had) dropped
supply	supplied	(has, have, had) supplied

Clint **has** practiced for the rodeo.
The cowhands **have** helped him.

A Draw one line under each helping verb and two lines under each main verb.

1. Slim Sanders had announced the start of the rodeo.

2. Horses had carried the riders around the ring.

3. The riders have practiced for a long time.

4. Our friend Clint has hopped onto his horse.

5. We have admired the parade of handsome horses.

6. Now the first event of the rodeo has started.

B Write *has* or *have* and the past form of the verb in parentheses to complete each sentence.

7. Rosa _____ the barrel race. **(enter)**

8. A horse _____ out of the gate. **(charge)**

9. The horses _____ away from the riders. **(hurry)**

10. Rosa _____ the reins into her hand. **(slip)**

11. She _____ toward the first barrel. **(race)**

12. The other cowhands _____ her speed. **(envy)**

13. Rosa _____ the blue ribbon. **(receive)**

14. Many people _____ eagerly for her. **(clap)**

15. We _____ the other contests too. **(watch)**

16. I _____ my day at the rodeo. **(enjoy)**

(continued)

© Houghton Mifflin Harcourt Publishing Company

Grade 4: Unit 3 Verbs *(Use with pupil book pages 110–111.)*
Skill: Students will identify main verbs and helping verbs and will form the perfect tenses.

Name _____

7 The Past with Helping Verbs (continued from page 50)

Challenge

The rodeo is about to begin! Show the cowhands which steers go into each corral. Read the sentence on each steer. Choose *have* or *has* to complete each sewntence correctly. Then write the sentence in the proper corral.

People ___?___ carried flags.

The rodeo ___?___ started.

Judges ___?___ awarded prizes.

Riders ___?___ grabbed the reins.

A man ___?___ closed the gate.

Horses ___?___ raced around barrels.

A cowhand ___?___ hurried to his horse.

The audience ___?___ clapped loudly.

HAS

1. _____

2. _____

3. _____

4. _____

HAVE

5. _____

6. _____

7. _____

8. _____

Writing Application: A Story

 EXPRESSING

Suppose that you are a cowhand. You and some other cowhands have tried out for a rodeo. Write a story about the tryout. Use the helping verbs *has, have,* and *had* with verbs in the past. Underline the helping verbs and circle the main verbs.

Grade 4: Unit 3 Verbs *(Use with pupil book pages 110–111.)*
Skill: Students will use the helping verbs *has, have,* and *had* correctly.

WORKBOOK PLUS
TCAP PRACTICE **51**

8 Irregular Verbs

Present	Past	Past with Helping Verbs
eat	ate	(has, have, had) eaten
give	gave	(has, have, had) given
make	made	(has, have, had) made

A Write the correct form of the verb in parentheses to complete each sentence.

1. I _____ my singing career at the age of ten. **(begin)**

2. My brother _____ me to a radio station. **(drive)**

3. He _____ his guitar with him. **(bring)**

4. I had _____ my song with me. **(bring)**

5. I had _____ it at home many times for practice. **(sing)**

6. I _____ all the words. **(know)**

7. I _____ the station director about my song. **(tell)**

8. Then I _____ it for her in a loud voice. **(sing)**

9. Soon a record company _____ a recording of my song. **(make)**

B 10–15. This radio announcement has six incorrect irregular verb forms. Use proofreading marks to correct the announcement.

Example: Ima Singer's songs have ~~broke~~ ᴬ many sales records.
broken

Proofreading Marks	
¶	Indent
∧	Add
﹏	Delete
≡	Capital letter
/	Small letter

NEWS FLASH!

Ima Singer's new CD camed out last week. Its sales

have grew very fast. It has took only days to reach

number one. Some people have says that this is her best CD ever.

Recently, the recording company threw a huge party for Ima.

They give her a special award. The thrill has not yet weared off.

(continued)

52 WORKBOOK PLUS
TCAP PRACTICE

Grade 4: Unit 3 Verbs *(Use with pupil book pages 112–113.)*
Skill: Students will write the past and past participle forms of irregular verbs.

Name _____

8 Irregular Verbs *(continued from page 52)*

Challenge

Unscramble the irregular verbs below, and write them in the blanks.
Then use some of these verbs to complete the songs below.

_____

_____   edma

_____   eta   evrod   _____

_____   erwo   otok   _____

                           moec   gruthob   _____

                           adis   wronth   _____

                                  erbok

"WINTER SONG"   "LUNCH TIME"

The wind _____ noises   When I went to school, I
outside.   _____ a huge lunch.

Small animals rushed to hide.   When I became hungry, I certainly

The trees _____ white caps.   _____ a bunch!

Bears prepared for long naps.

Winter had _____ at last.

Now, on another piece of paper, write your own song. Give your song a title.
Use at least two more verbs from the above list.

Writing Application: A Song

EXPRESSING

Suppose that you are a songwriter. Write five sentences that you would
like to use in a new song. Use a verb from the Word Box in each sentence.
Remember to use the helping verbs *has, have,* and *had* where they are needed.

brought	eaten	given	known	told
drove	gave	knew	made	wore

Grade 4: Unit 3 Verbs *(Use with pupil book pages 112–113.)*
Skill: Students will use the past and past perfect tenses of irregular verbs.

WORKBOOK PLUS
TCAP PRACTICE   53

Name _____

9 The Special Verb *be*

Present Tense	Past Tense
My <u>mother</u> **is** in court.	A <u>man</u> **was** there.
<u>We</u> **are** with her.	Many <u>people</u> **were** in court.

A Underline the verb in each sentence. Then write *past* or *present* for each verb.

1. My mother is a judge.   _____

2. She was the first woman judge in our town.   _____

3. Now there are more women judges.   _____

4. Last week we were in her court.   _____

5. It was so interesting!   _____

6. People are in court to solve problems.   _____

B 7–12. The following is a section of Kendra's personal essay. Use proofreading marks to correct six mistakes in the form of the verb *be*.

Example: We ~~was~~ ^were^ with our mother in court.

Proofreading Marks
¶   Indent
∧   Add
ℐ   Delete
≡   Capital letter
/   Small letter

Yesterday my sister and I was in court with my mom.

She was a judge. Many people was watching her with respect. We was so proud

of her! That night after dinner, she asked us to wash the dishes.

I said, "No way, Mom! We was already watching TV." She gave me that look.

"Okay," I said. "Now I know why you like your job."

"Why?" She were smiling now.

"Everyone always does what you say!" I replied.

(continued)

Grade 4: Unit 3   Verbs   *(Use with pupil book pages 114–115.)*
Skill: Students will identify and will use present and past tense forms of the verb *be*.

Name _____

9 The Special Verb *be* (continued from page 54)

Challenge

Suppose that you are in a courtroom. Use the verb *is* or *are* to complete the sentences describing the picture below.

1. The judge _____ in her large leather chair.

2. A wooden gavel _____ on her desk.

3. Six jury members _____ near the judge.

4. They _____ quiet but alert.

Now suppose that you are back in your classroom. You have seen the judge solve "The Case of the Missing Wig." Tell your classmates and teacher what happened. Use a past tense form of the verb *be* in each sentence.

5. _____

6. _____

7. _____

8. _____

Writing Application: An Opinion

EXPRESSING

You are a judge. Someone has invented a new toy. Mr. Glurg says that he invented it. Miss Plish says that she invented it. You must decide who the inventor really is. Write six sentences that give your opinion on this important case. Use a form of the verb *be* in each sentence.

Grade 4: Unit 3 Verbs *(Use with pupil book pages 114–115.)*
Skill: Students will write present and past tense forms of the verb *be*.

WORKBOOK PLUS
TCAP PRACTICE 55

Name _____

10 Contractions with *not*

Two Words	Contraction
We **do not** have rules.	We **don't** have rules.
It **is not** easy to make them.	It **isn't** easy to make them.
Fred **will not** help.	Fred **won't** help.

A Write a contraction for the word or words in parentheses.

1. My old club _____ made any rules. **(had not)**

2. Our new club _____ made rules either. **(has not)**

3. I _____ like the club meetings. **(do not)**

4. The members _____ listening to each other. **(are not)**

5. Several members _____ even at the last meeting. **(were not)**

6. We _____ get anything done. **(cannot)**

7. We _____ agreed to anyone's ideas. **(have not)**

8. Club members _____ have to guess the rules. **(should not)**

B Underline the contraction in each sentence. Write the word or words that make up each contraction.

9. You wouldn't like this club. _____

10. Wally and Inga won't join the club. _____

11. They didn't enjoy the first meeting. _____

12. Wally couldn't say his ideas. _____

13. People weren't listening to him. _____

14. Wasn't that a rude way to act? _____

15. Doesn't anyone else want some rules? _____

16. It isn't so hard to make them. _____

17. Why shouldn't it work? _____

18. People don't like too many rules. _____

(continued)

Grade 4: Unit 3   Verbs   *(Use with pupil book pages 116–117.)*
Skill: Students will form contractions with *not*.

Name _____

10 Contractions with *not* (continued from page 56)

Challenge

Clever Cleaver posted the following rules in the lunchroom. Cleaver's rules don't make sense. Rewrite each rule, using a contraction with *not*. Then write three more lunchroom rules. Use a contraction with *not* in each rule.

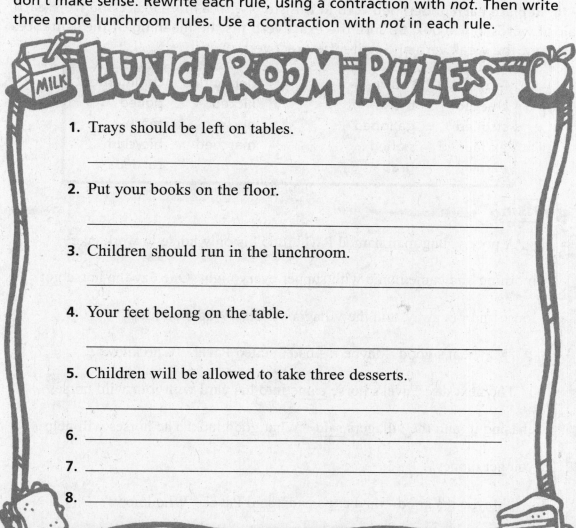

LUNCHROOM RULES

1. Trays should be left on tables.

_____

2. Put your books on the floor.

_____

3. Children should run in the lunchroom.

_____

4. Your feet belong on the table.

_____

5. Children will be allowed to take three desserts.

_____

6. _____

7. _____

8. _____

Writing Application: Rules

EXPLAINING

You and some friends have formed the Bicycle Safety Club. Make up five bicycle safety rules that club members should follow. Use a contraction with *not* in each rule.

Grade 4: Unit 3 Verbs *(Use with pupil book pages 116–117.)*
Skill: Students will form contractions with *not*.

WORKBOOK PLUS
TCAP PRACTICE **57**

Name _____

Using Exact Verbs

> *owned*
> The woman and her son ~~had~~ only a poor shack and a horse.

1–10. Replace each underlined verb in this story with a more exact one from each pair of words in the box. Be sure the exact verb fits the meaning of the sentence. Cross out the weak verb and write the exact verb over it.

left	returned	demanded	commented
cracked	broke	kicked	poked
strolled	galloped	nurse	teach
exclaimed	sighed	marched	bicycled
earn	grab	won	carried

Revising

A poor young man named Pavel rode his only horse to work every morning and <u>came</u> home with supper every night. One day the horse <u>got</u> loose and ran away, and the villagers cried, "What bad luck!"

"Maybe it's good. Maybe it's bad," <u>stated</u> Pavel. "Who knows?"

The next day, Pavel's horse <u>came</u> into his yard with four wild horses chasing it, and the villagers <u>said</u>, "What good luck! The horses will help you <u>get</u> money."

"Maybe it's good. Maybe it's bad," <u>said</u> Pavel. "Who knows?"

The next day, one wild horse <u>hit</u> Pavel and broke his leg, and the villagers cried, "What bad luck! Now your mother must <u>help</u> you."

The next day, soldiers <u>came</u> into the village and <u>took</u> every healthy man off to meet the king, but they did not take Pavel. Was it good luck or bad luck?

Grade 4: Unit 3 Verbs *(Use with pupil book page 118.)*
Skill: Students will replace weak verbs with exact verbs.

Name _____

1 What Is an Adjective?

| What kind | China is a **huge** country with a **long, interesting** history. |
| How many | **Many** people live in China. |

A Write the adjectives that describe the underlined nouns. Then write *what kind* or *how many* for each adjective.

1. The main <u>language</u> in China is Chinese.

_____

2. Some <u>people</u> in China can read several foreign <u>languages</u> too.

_____

3. There are many <u>ways</u> to speak Chinese.

_____

4. People in separate <u>villages</u> may use different <u>words</u>.

_____

B Write each adjective and the noun that it describes.

5. Chinese is written in special symbols called characters.

_____

6. One small character can stand for a whole idea.

_____

7. There are over a thousand characters.

_____

8. People write the characters with black ink and fine brushes.

_____

9. The characters look like pretty, delicate pictures.

_____

10. The characters appear on many ancient paintings.

_____

(continued)

Grade 4: Unit 4 Adjectives *(Use with pupil book pages 136–137.)*
Skill: Students will identify adjectives and the nouns that they modify.

WORKBOOK PLUS
TCAP PRACTICE

59

Name _____

1 What Is an Adjective? *(continued from page 59)*

Challenge

The Chinese are famous not only for their beautiful writing but also for their beautiful paintings and drawings. Look at these examples of Chinese-style drawings. Then write three sentences to describe each one. Use adjectives that tell *what kind* and *how many*.

1. _____

2. _____

3. _____

4. _____

5. _____

6. _____

Writing Application: A Journal Entry

DESCRIBING

You are traveling in a foreign country. You don't speak the people's language, and they don't speak English. Write five sentences about your first day in this country. Describe the problems that you face and how you solve them. Use adjectives that tell *what kind* or *how many* in each sentence.

Grade 4: Unit 4 Adjectives *(Use with pupil book pages 136–137.)*
Skill: Students will use adjectives in sentences.

Name _____

Writing with Adjectives

> **huge, trumpeting**   **center**
> The circus elephants marched into the ring.
>   ∧   ∧

Elaborating Sentences 1–8. Rewrite this letter. Use adjectives to elaborate each underlined sentence.

Revising

Dear Aunt Sally,

   We went to the circus last night. <u>I laughed when the clown stumbled.</u> He pretended he could not get up. <u>In the middle ring, acrobats rode a bicycle.</u> The tightrope walker was high overhead. <u>She held an umbrella for balance.</u> Next, the ringmaster blew a whistle. <u>Horses raced into the ring.</u> <u>Each horse carried a rider.</u> The riders did tricks while the horses galloped.

   Then circus workers put up a safety net. <u>High above, the trapeze artists performed.</u> The most exciting act was next. <u>A daredevil was shot out of a cannon.</u> <u>The circus ended with a parade.</u> What a great time we had!

   Your nephew,
   Sam

(continued)

Grade 4: Unit 4   Adjectives   *(Use with pupil book pages 138–139.)*
Skill: Students will elaborate sentences with adjectives.

**WORKBOOK PLUS
TCAP PRACTICE** 61

Name _____

Writing with Adjectives *(continued from page 61)*

Not combined	We bought cotton candy at the circus. The cotton candy was pink.
Combined	We bought pink cotton candy at the circus.

Combining Sentences 9–16. Rewrite this e-mail message, combining each pair of underlined sentences.

Revising

e-mail

To: Rena
From: Max
Subject: The Circus

   I rode a camel at the circus. The camel was tan. Its legs were long. Its legs were skinny. To get on the camel, I climbed a ladder. The ladder was tall. Then I stepped onto the camel's back. I rode in a saddle. The saddle was leather. A blanket covered the saddle. The blanket was wool.

   The camel's name was Whitney. Whitney had big eyes. Her eyes were brown. I rode Whitney around a ring. The ring was small. The ride was bumpy. The ride was fun.

_____

_____

_____

_____

_____

_____

_____

_____

_____

Grade 4: Unit 4 Adjectives *(Use with pupil book pages 138–139.)*
Skill: Students will combine sentences by moving adjectives.

Name _____

2 Adjectives After *be*

The weather <u>was</u> **awful**.	The lakes <u>were</u> **frozen**.
It <u>is</u> **cold**.	They <u>are</u> **slippery** now.

Write each adjective and the word that it describes.

1. Finally, the sky was clear. _____

2. The winds are cold on our faces. _____

3. I am chilly. _____

4. The snow is fluffy like cotton. _____

5. It is deep everywhere. _____

6. Plows were busy on our street. _____

7. They are noisy. _____

8. Snowstorms are exciting! _____

Challenge

You have invented a wonderful new snow shovel called the Super Shovel. Complete this advertisement for the Super Shovel. Use an adjective in each sentence. The adjective must follow a form of the verb *be*.

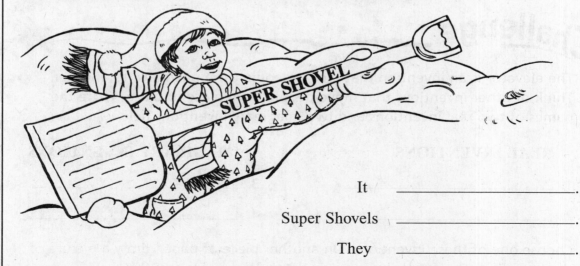

It _____.

Super Shovels _____.

They _____.

Grade 4: Unit 4 Adjectives (Use with pupil book page 140.)
Skill: Students will identify and will use predicate adjectives.

WORKBOOK PLUS
TCAP PRACTICE 63

© Houghton Mifflin Harcourt Publishing Company

Name _____

3 Using *a*, *an*, and *the*

A B C D   Jacob is **a** good student.
He knows how to use **an** encyclopedia.
He finds **the** correct volume and **the** right pages.   **W X Y Z**

Write the correct article in parentheses to complete each sentence.

1. Jacob is writing _____ report. (**a, an**)

2. It is about _____ famous inventor. (**a, an**)

3. Elisha Otis invented _____ elevator. (**a, the**)

4. In Otis's day, _____ building could not be very tall. (**a, an**)

5. Walking up _____ stairs was tiring. (**a, the**)

6. _____ elevator changed all that. (**A, The**)

7. Jacob used _____ encyclopedia for his report. (**a, an**)

8. He took out _____ volume marked *O*. (**an, the**)

9. Jacob found _____ article about Otis. (**a, an**)

10. He also looked for information about _____ elevator. (**a, the**)

11. Jacob made notes on _____ piece of paper. (**a, an**)

Challenge

The elevator is an invention that moves people from one place to another. Think of other inventions that move people from place to place. Write the names of two real inventions and two imaginary inventions below.

REAL INVENTIONS   **IMAGINARY INVENTIONS**

1. _____   3. _____

2. _____   4. _____

Choose one of these inventions. On another piece of paper, draw a picture of the invention. Then describe it, using the articles *a, an,* and *the.*

Grade 4: Unit 4   Adjectives   (*Use with pupil book page 141.*)
Skill: Students will use articles correctly.

4 Making Comparisons

Adjective	Comparing Two	Comparing Three or More
old	old**er**	old**est**
large	larg**er**	larg**est**
big	bi**gger**	bi**ggest**
lazy	laz**ier**	laz**iest**

A Write the correct form of the adjective in parentheses to complete each sentence.

1. Collecting stamps is the _____ way of all to learn about them. **(easy)**

2. The _____ stamp ever used on mail was made in 1840. **(old)**

3. The _____ of all postage stamps sold for one cent. **(early)**

4. Mounting stamps with a tool is _____ than using your fingers. **(wise)**

5. The tool with the _____ point of all works best. **(thin)**

B 6–10. This part of an article on stamp collecting has five incorrect forms of adjectives with *-er* and *-est*. Use proofreading marks to correct the adjectives.

Example: The ~~poorer~~ stamp of all is one that is torn.
                        poorest

Proofreading Marks

¶	Indent
∧	Add
℉	Delete
≡	Capital letter
/	Small letter

Proofreading

The rarer stamp in the world is known as the 1856

one-cent British Guiana magenta. It does not look very special. It is

tiny than many other stamps. Other rare stamps are also pretty and

bright than the one-cent magenta. It is not the older one, either. Still,

it was sold for almost one million dollars because it is one of a kind.

That makes the one-cent magenta truly the rarest stamp of all.

(continued)

Grade 4: Unit 4   Adjectives   *(Use with pupil book pages 142–143.)*   **WORKBOOK PLUS**   **65**
   Skill: Students will form and will use the comparative and the superlative   **TCAP PRACTICE**
        forms of adjectives.

Name _____

4 Making Comparisons (continued from page 65)

Challenge

Add -*er* or -*est* to an adjective from the Word Box to complete each sentence. The sentences are clues about a mystery word.

r̲ich	pretty	s̲unny	bright	o̲ld
fast	e̲asy	l̲ittle	h̲igh	n̲ear

1. It's the _____ thing of all to give.

2. It's the _____ of all sunny days.

3. It is _____ than lightning.

4. It's the _____ gift of all.

5. It is _____ than the moon.

6. The _____ child of all can give it.

7. It's _____ than you think.

8. It's the _____ thing around.

9. It's _____ of all when it's very old.

10. It's _____ than a shining light.

Now unscramble the underlined letters in the Word Box to discover the mystery word.

_____

Writing Application: A Description

COMPARING AND CONTRASTING

You have been chosen to design three new stamps for the United States. Write six sentences that describe and compare your stamps. Use adjectives with -*er* and -*est* in at least four of your sentences.

Grade 4: Unit 4   Adjectives   *(Use with pupil book pages 142–143.)*
Skill: Students will form and will use the comparative and the superlative forms of adjectives.

© Houghton Mifflin Harcourt Publishing Company

Name _____

5 Comparing with *more* and *most*

> Daisies are **plentiful** flowers.
> Violets are **more plentiful** than day lilies.
> Are dandelions the **most plentiful** flowers of all?

A Write the correct form of the adjective in parentheses to complete each sentence.

1. Are wildflowers the _____ of all plants? **(interesting)**

2. Seeing flowers is _____ than reading about them. **(pleasant)**

3. Certain flowers are _____ than others. **(numerous)**

4. Dandelions are _____ in spring than in fall. **(plentiful)**

5. I think the rose is the _____ flower of all. **(beautiful)**

B 6–10. This part of an interview has five missing or incorrect uses of the words *more* and *most*. Use proofreading marks to correct the interview.

Example: Some flower names sound ~~most~~ *more* scientific than others.

Proofreading

Proofreading Marks	
¶	Indent
∧	Add
℘	Delete
☰	Capital letter
/	Small letter

Reporter: What is the popularest occasion to send flowers?

Florist: Well, it's pretty close, but I think Valentine's

Day is more busier than Mother's Day.

R: What is your more favorite flower of all?

F: I think the white peonies in my garden are most precious than

the other flowers.

R: What is the most difficult part of your job?

F: The most hardest thing is to keep flowers fresh.

(continued)

Grade 4: Unit 4   Adjectives   *(Use with pupil book pages 144–145.)*
 Skill: Students will use *more* and *most* to form the comparative and the
 superlative forms of adjectives.

WORKBOOK PLUS
TCAP PRACTICE

67

Name _____

5 Comparing with *more* and *most* (continued from page 67)

Challenge

Write a sentence to describe each of the imaginary flowers below. Use adjectives with *more* or *most* in each description.

whisker rose

gloomy-gus willow bud

1. _____

_____

_____

3. _____

_____

_____

freckle-face primrose

sweet-and-sour lily

2. _____

_____

_____

4. _____

_____

_____

On another piece of paper, draw two imaginary flowers. Give each flower a name. Then write a sentence, describing each flower. Use adjectives with *more* and *most* in your descriptions.

Writing Application: A Post Card

DESCRIBING

You are on a safari in a tropical jungle. Unusual flowers bloom all over the jungle. Write a post card to a relative, telling about the flowers that you have seen. In each sentence, use adjectives with *more* or *most*.

Grade 4: Unit 4 Adjectives *(Use with pupil book pages 144–145.)*
Skill: Students will use *more* and *most* to form the comparative and the superlative forms of adjectives.

6 Comparing with *good* and *bad*

> Cindy is a **good** driver.
> Kay is a **better** driver than Cindy.
> Shula is the **best** driver I know.
>
> That road is **bad**.
> This road is **worse** than that road.
> Our road is the **worst** of all.

A Write each sentence correctly. Use the correct form of the adjective in parentheses.

1. Taking lessons is the ____ way of all to learn to drive. **(good)**

2. Learning from a teacher is ____ than learning on your own. **(good)**

3. A nervous person makes a ____ teacher than a calm one. **(bad)**

4. Teaching yourself is the ____ way of all to learn to drive. **(bad)**

B 5–10. Use proofreading marks to correct six incorrect forms of the adjectives *good* and *bad* in the e-mail message below.

Example: The ~~worse~~ worst mistake of all is drinking alcohol and driving.

Proofreading — e-mail

I helped my sister study for her driving exam. Here are my most good tips:

• It is best to go the speed limit than to go more slowly.

• The roads are more bad when it snows than when it rains.

• Wet roads are worse, but icy roads are worst of all for driving.

• Air bags are good for safety, but seat belts are the most best.

• Even slow driving is gooder than careless driving.

Proofreading Marks
¶ Indent
∧ Add
ℐ Delete
≡ Capital letter
/ Small letter

(continued)

Name _____

6 Comparing with *good* and *bad* (continued from page 69)

Challenge

You are a car dealer, and you are trying to sell the cars shown below. Tell your customers about each car by comparing them. Complete each sentence, using a form of the adjective *good* or *bad*.

1. The four-door model is _____ .

2. The two-door model is _____ .

3. The sports car is _____ .

4. The racer is _____ .

5. The yellow van is _____ .

Design your own car of the future. On another piece of paper, draw a picture of your car. Then write five sentences, explaining why your car will be better than cars of today. Use a form of *good* or *bad* in each sentence you write.

6. _____

7. _____

8. _____

9. _____

10. _____

Writing Application: A Story

Finish this story. Use forms of the adjectives *good* and *bad* in your sentences. Yesterday started out like any other day. The bus stopped at the corner, and I got on. That turned out to be the worst bus ride I ever had! This is what happened. . . .

Grade 4: Unit 4   Adjectives   (*Use with pupil book pages 146–147.*)
Skill: Students will use the comparative and the superlative forms of *good* and *bad*.

Name _____

Using Exact Adjectives

>   **crimson**   **glistening**
> I like the ~~nice~~ sunsets and the ~~shiny~~ ocean at Fort Pierce, Florida.

1–10. Replace each underlined adjective in this part of a story with a more exact adjective from each pair of words in the box. Be sure the exact adjective fits the meaning of the sentence. Cross out the weak adjective and write the exact adjective above it.

sunlit	dreary		firm	determined
fat	vast		banging	thunderous
twinkling	dull		ordinary	salty
short	tiny		parched	wet
foaming	soapy		perfect	large

Revising

The pearl fisher squints at the bright surface of the ocean. He thinks the ocean looks like a big tub of shiny stars. He imagines that the ocean is teasing him with thousands of small winks. He can almost hear the white waves shouting, "Go home!" The strong pearl fisher ignores the ocean's loud warning.

He licks the strange taste of the waves off his dry lips. He knows that today he will find that great black pearl.

Grade 4: Unit 4 Adjectives *(Use with pupil book page 148.)*
Skill: Students will replace weak adjectives with more exact adjectives.

WORKBOOK PLUS
TCAP PRACTICE

71

Name _____

1 Correct Sentences

Run-on	Movies are fun to watch do you like them too?
Correct	Movies are fun to watch. **Do** you like them too?
Statement	Movies are fun to watch.
Question	Have you ever seen one being made?
Command	Tell me about it, please.
Exclamation	What a wonderful experience that must be!

Write these sentences correctly. Add capital letters and end marks.
Write each run-on sentence as two sentences.

1. do you like old movies

_____

2. some old movies were made without sound how funny the actors look

_____

_____

3. my favorite movie star of silent films is Mary Pickford

_____

4. did directors of old movies use more than one camera

_____

5. how strange movies would be without modern equipment

_____

6. please describe the movie camera tell how it was invented

_____

7. do you know about special effects explain them to me, please

_____

_____

8. computers can create unusual pictures have you seen any

_____

(continued)

Grade 4: Unit 5   Capitalization and Punctuation   *(Use with pupil book pages 166–167.)*
    Skill: Students will capitalize and punctuate sentences and will correct run-on
        sentences.

1 Correct Sentences (continued from page 72)

Challenge

In a movie script, the characters' words are written in sentences called lines. Look at each movie scene below. Write the lines for each character. The word in parentheses tells what kind of sentence to write.

SCENE ONE

Guard: *(Command)* _____

Boy: *(Question)* _____

Guard: *(Statement)* _____

Girl: *(Exclamation)* _____

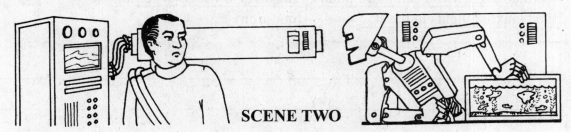

SCENE TWO

Man: *(Question)* _____

Robot: *(Command)* _____

Man: *(Exclamation)* _____

Robot: *(Statement)* _____

Writing Application: A Review

Think of one of your favorite movies. Decide why you like it so much. Write six sentences to describe the best parts of this movie. Include a statement, a question, a command, and an exclamation. Be sure to use capital letters and end marks correctly.

Name _____

Writing Good Sentences

| One type of sentence | I like to look at the stars. I always look for the North Star. Once I saw a shooting star. I thought it was beautiful. |
| Different types of sentences | Have you ever noticed how many brilliant stars you can see? Look for the North Star. Once I saw a shooting star. It was so beautiful! |

Writing Different Types of Sentences 1–6. Rewrite this science article. Change each underlined statement to a question, a command, or an exclamation. The word in parentheses will tell you which kind of sentence to write.

Revising

When the sun goes down, the night lights come up. This is a beautiful sight to see. (exclamation) First, you might spend some time looking at the moon. (command) Moonlight is sunlight reflected off the moon. Then you can move on to the twinkling lights in the sky.

(command) The twinkling lights are stars. Some of the stars we see are more than 2.5 million light-years away. (exclamation) You may notice pinpoints of light that do not twinkle. (question) They are planets. The night sky is so beautiful. (question)

1. _____

2. _____

3. _____

4. _____

5. _____

6. _____

(continued)

Grade 4: Unit 5 Capitalization and Punctuation *(Use with pupil book pages 168–169.)*
Skill: Students will rewrite statements, changing them to questions, commands, and exclamations.

Name _____

Writing Good Sentences *(continued from page 74)*

Two sentences	We have studied comets. We know a lot about them.
Compound sentence	We have studied comets, **and** we know a lot about them.
Compound predicate	We have studied comets **and** know a lot about them.

Combining Sentences 7–12. Rewrite each underlined pair of sentences in this script. First, combine the two sentences to form a compound sentence. Then combine them to form a sentence with a compound predicate.

Revising

Professor Starr

I know all about comets. I can tell you about them. Comets appear suddenly in the sky. They are rock-and-ice balls. They have a tail of gas and dust. Reflected sunlight makes the tail of the comet glow.

Professor Knight

Well, do you know what a meteor is? It is a rock from space. It enters Earth's atmosphere at high speed. Most meteors burn up when they hit the atmosphere. Some crash into the ground.

7. Compound Sentence: _____

_____

8. Compound Predicate: _____

_____

9. Compound Sentence: _____

_____

10. Compound Predicate: _____

_____

11. Compound Sentence: _____

_____

12. Compound Predicate: _____

Grade 4: Unit 5   Capitalization and Punctuation *(Use with pupil book pages 168–169.)*   **WORKBOOK PLUS** **TCAP PRACTICE**   **75**
   Skill: Students will combine sentences to form compound sentences and
      sentences with a compound predicate.

Name _____

2 Capitalizing Names of People and Pets

People and pets	David Mazur has a bird named Bert.
Titles and initials	R. U. Shure voted for Mayor Rita Day.
Family titles	Uncle Milt and my grandfather are here.

Write these sentences correctly. Add capital letters where they are needed.

1. Pets like my dog folger can help people in many ways.

   _____

2. My neighbor sara enos lives alone.

   _____

3. Her cat, liza, keeps her from feeling lonely.

   _____

4. Even dr. a. j. sills says that pets can help people's health.

   _____

5. His cat, pootzer, helps keep him calm.

   _____

6. Some blind people, like mrs. gina l. petri, have guide dogs.

   _____

7. Monkeys are trained by ms. carole wu to help deaf people.

   _____

8. Today aunt paula told me about a special law for older people.

   _____

9. The law was suggested by senator w. proxmire.

   _____

10. It would allow my grandpa to keep his dog, bo, in his apartment.

    _____

(continued)

Grade 4: Unit 5 Capitalization and Punctuation *(Use with pupil book pages 170–171.)*
Skill: Students will capitalize proper nouns.

Name _____

2 Capitalizing Names of People and Pets (continued from page 76)

Challenge _____

Some people say that dog owners and their dogs look alike. Look at the pictures of these dogs and their owners. Then write a name for each pet owner and pet. The first one has been done for you.

1. **Miss Patty Paris**

   Frenchy

3. _____

   _____

2. _____

   _____

4. _____

   _____

Now choose one pet and owner and write three sentences to describe them. Capitalize names correctly in your sentences.

5. _____

6. _____

7. _____

Writing Application: A Report

EXPLAINING

   Suppose that you are an animal doctor. Today six people brought their pets to you. Write a sentence about each pet owner and what you did to help his or her pet. Use the name of a person and a pet in each sentence.

© Houghton Mifflin Harcourt Publishing Company

Grade 4: Unit 5   Capitalization and Punctuation   *(Use with pupil book pages 170–171.)*
   Skill: Students will capitalize proper nouns.

**WORKBOOK PLUS
TCAP PRACTICE**   **77**

Name _____

3 Names of Places and Things

> Is the Fourth of July the first Monday in July?
> We drove from Toledo, Ohio, to the Pocono Mountains.
> The Bourse Building and Peace Park are on Ridge Road.
> The Glee Club flew across the Atlantic Ocean to France.

A Write these sentences correctly. Add capital letters where they are needed.

1. Tim Farad spent the months of march and april in new zealand.

   _____

2. He visited the city of auckland near hauraki gulf one wednesday.

   _____

3. He also visited mount cook and fiordland national park.

   _____

4. He heard the new zealand symphony orchestra play last friday.

   _____

B 5–14. This post card has ten missing capital letters in names of places and things. Use proofreading marks to correct the errors.

Example: Tim enjoyed visiting the national library of new zealand.

Proofreading

Dear Aunt Rosa,

   Greetings from across the Pacific ocean!

I love new zealand! Last sunday I went to a concert

in the capital city of Wellington. Tomorrow is anzac

day. In may I will fly back to california and our home on

sandy road. See you soon!

                                        Love,

                                        Tim

Proofreading Marks	
¶	Indent
∧	Add
℈	Delete
☰	Capital letter
/	Small letter

(continued)

© Houghton Mifflin Harcourt Publishing Company

3 Names of Places and Things (continued from page 78)

Challenge

Complete this letter, using real or made-up names. Your letter can be serious or funny. Sign your name at the bottom. Be sure to use capital letters where they are needed.

_____
(date)

Dear _____
(friend's name)

Hi! I'm spending the months of _____ and

_____ in the state of _____. We are near

a lake. It is named _____, but it should be named

_____ because _____.

My brother and I climbed a mountain. We would like to change the mountain's

name from _____ to _____ because

_____.

On the holiday of _____, we will visit a big building called

the _____. It looks like _____.

Your friend,

_____
(your name)

Writing Application: A Letter

DESCRIBING

You have a pen pal in New Zealand. Write a letter to your friend, describing the place where you live. Mention interesting places such as rivers, mountains, lakes, buildings, and parks. Be sure to write the day and the month at the top of your letter.

Grade 4: Unit 5 Capitalization and Punctuation (Use with pupil book pages 172–173.)
Skill: Students will capitalize proper nouns.

WORKBOOK PLUS
TCAP PRACTICE
79

Name _____

4 Abbreviations

Titles	Doctor	**Dr.**	Senior	**Sr.**
Addresses	Road	**Rd.**	Company	**Co.**
Months	March	**Mar.**	November	**Nov.**
Days	Tuesday	**Tues.**	Saturday	**Sat.**
States	Alabama	**AL**	Wisconsin	**WI**

A Write these groups of words, using correct abbreviations.

1. Wednesday, October 11 _____

2. Mister Roberto Perez Junior _____

3. a married woman named Eva Dansk _____

4. 24 Ashley Road, Augusta, Maine _____

5. Post Office Box 101 _____

6. Fuzzy Top Hat Company _____

7. Saturday, February 28 _____

B Write each address. Use an abbreviation for each underlined word.

8. <u>Mister</u> Marcel Field <u>Senior</u> _____

   100 Viola <u>Avenue</u> _____

   Haddonfield, <u>New Jersey</u> 08033 _____

9. Arno Book <u>Company</u> _____

   Cross Bay <u>Boulevard</u> _____

   Brooklyn, <u>New York</u> 11214 _____

10. <u>Doctor</u> Sue Belsky _____

    15 Kerwood <u>Drive</u> _____

    Wayne, <u>Pennsylvania</u> 19087 _____

(continued)

Grade 4: Unit 5   Capitalization and Punctuation   *(Use with pupil book pages 174–175.)*
Skill: Students will write abbreviations correctly.

4 Abbreviations (continued from page 80)

Challenge

Complete the crossword puzzle below. First, find the abbreviation in each clue. Then write the word or words that the abbreviation stands for.

ACROSS

1. Jan. 6, 1987
3. Wed. afternoon
6. Belmar, NJ 07719
9. Sanderson, FL 32087
11. Oct. 22, 1980
12. Dec. 15, 1971
13. Gary, IN 46401
14. Aug. 2, 1989
15. Kiddie Kite Co.

DOWN

1. Robert Top Jr.
2. 212 Gribble Ave.
4. Dr. Yolanda Korbit
5. Jeffrey Giomo Sr.
7. 79–A Fern St.
8. Rebel Rd.
9. Fri., May 14
10. Twin Falls, ID 83301

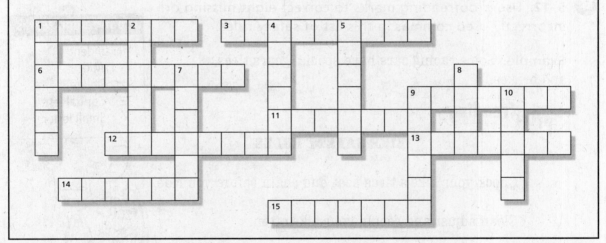

Writing Application: An Invitation

Write an invitation for a party you are giving. Include the month, the day, and the time of the party. Write the address of the place where it will be held. Then write the names and the addresses of three people you want to invite. Use correct abbreviations.

Grade 4: Unit 5   Capitalization and Punctuation   *(Use with pupil book pages 174–175.)*
Skill: Students will write abbreviations and the words that they stand for.

WORKBOOK PLUS TCAP PRACTICE

81

Name _____

5 Commas in a Series

Bicycling is good for <u>exercise, fun, and transportation</u>.
A new rider learns to <u>pedal, turn, and stop</u> a bike.

A Write these sentences correctly. Add commas where they are needed.

1. Many adults teens and children love bicycling.

   _____

2. Riders should respect learn and obey safety rules.

   _____

3. Find out the bicycle rules for your town county and state.

   _____

4. Always oil tighten and inspect the parts of your bike.

   _____

B 5–12. Use proofreading marks to correct eight missing or incorrectly used commas in this list of safety rules.

Example: Some racing cars have special gears, tires, and brakes.

Proofreading Marks	
¶	Indent
∧	Add
⌥	Delete
≡	Capital letter
/	Small letter

Proofreading

BIKE SAFETY RULES

• Check your bike's tires seat and chain before you ride.

• Clean adjust and repair, your bike often.

• Always use a horn light and reflectors after dusk.

• Avoid carrying packages, passengers, and animals, on your bike.

• Wear a helmet and signal when you ride your bike on public roads.

(continued)

Grade 4: Unit 5 Capitalization and Punctuation *(Use with pupil book pages 176–177.)*
Skill: Students will use commas in a series.

Name _____

5 Commas in a Series (continued from page 82)

Challenge

During the summer, you went on a bicycle trip with the Bicycle Buzzards Club. Here are four pictures you took on your trip. Beside each picture, write three words that tell about the picture.

Now tell what is happening in each picture in your photo album. Write sentences that use the groups of words you wrote above. Each sentence should have a series.

1. _____

2. _____

3. _____

4. _____

Writing Application: Biographical Nonfiction

Think of a new skill that you have learned, such as fishing, sewing, or playing an instrument. Write six sentences about how you learned this skill. Use a series of three words in each sentence.

Grade 4: Unit 5 Capitalization and Punctuation (Use with pupil book pages 176–177.)
  Skill: Students will use commas in a series.

WORKBOOK PLUS
TCAP PRACTICE

83

Name _____

Writing Good Sentences

Choppy sentences	Deer live in fields. Deer live in meadows. Deer live in woods.
Combined sentence	Deer live in fields, meadows, **and** woods.

Combining Sentences to Make a Series 1–5. Rewrite each underlined set of sentences in this report as one new sentence.

Revising

Bison belong to the same family as sheep. They belong to the same family as goats. Bison belong to the same family as cattle. Bison are also called buffalo. They have large heads and a hump between their shoulders. Bison's heads are covered by long, shaggy fur. Their necks are covered by long, shaggy fur. Their shoulders are covered by long, shaggy fur. Bison eat grass. Bison eat twigs. Bison eat leaves.

In the past, Native Americans hunted bison. They used every part of the animal. They used the bison's hide. They used the bison's meat. They used the bison's bones.

Today, bison are bred in zoos and on ranches. Then they are released into parks and refuges. Buffalo roam in parks in Wyoming. They roam in parks in Montana. They roam in parks in Canada.

1. _____

_____

2. _____

_____

3. _____

_____

4. _____

_____

5. _____

_____

(continued)

Grade 4: Unit 5 Capitalization and Punctuation (*Use with pupil book pages 178–179.*)
Skill: Students will combine sentences by joining single words in a series.

Name _____

Writing Good Sentences *(continued from page 84)*

Choppy sentences	Bluestem bunchgrass grows on the plains. Thin needlegrass grows on the plains. Tough wire grass grows on the plains.
Combined sentence	Bluestem bunchgrass, thin needlegrass, **and** tough wire grass grow on the plains.

Combining Sentences to Make a Series 6–10. Rewrite each set of underlined sentences in this video script as one sentence.

Revising

NARRATOR: The bison's habitat is the grassland of the Great Plains, but bison are not the only animals on the grasslands. Pronghorn antelope live there. Prairie dogs live there. Several kinds of rabbit live there too. Don't let the name "grassland" fool you. There are other plants besides grasses. Berry bushes grow in bison country. Small aspen trees grow in bison country. Wild roses grow in bison country. Many species of birds also live on the plains. There are prairie falcons. There are American kestrels. There are two kinds of owl. People have settled there too. Maxican colonists have lived there. Native Americans have lived there. Other settlers have lived there. Nowadays, residents of the Great Plains make a living from grain farming. They make a living from cattle ranching. They make a living from mineral products.

6. _____

_____

7. _____

_____

8. _____

_____

9. _____

_____

10. _____

_____

Grade 4: Unit 5 Capitalization and Punctuation *(Use with pupil book pages 178–179.)*
Skill: Students will combine sentences by joining phrases in a series.

**WORKBOOK PLUS
TCAP PRACTICE**

85

Name _____

6 More Uses for Commas

<u>Yes</u>, science is interesting.   <u>Chen</u>, name a great scientist.
<u>Well</u>, I like the experiments.   Was Madame Curie a scientist, <u>Julia</u>?

A Write each sentence correctly. Add commas where they are needed.

1. Chen what do you know about scientists of long ago?

_____

2. Well some early Greeks were good scientists.

_____

3. Did the Greeks also invent the compass Julia?

_____

4. No a Chinese scientist invented that.

_____

5–10. This interview has six missing commas. Use proofreading marks to correct the interview.

Example: Mr. Lopez: It's good to talk with you**,** Julia.

Proofreading Marks

¶	Indent
∧	Add
﹎	Delete
≡	Capital letter
/	Small letter

Proofreading

Mr. Lopez: Can you tell me Julia who invented a

way to lift water?

Julia: It was another Greek scientist Mr. Lopez.

Mr. Lopez: Yes, and why was that a helpful invention Julia?

Julia: Well, it helped farmers water their crops.

Mr. Lopez: Julia wasn't it a Chinese scientist who discovered

laws about levers and pulleys?

Julia: No actually it was the same Greek scientist.

(continued)

Name _____

6 More Uses for Commas (continued from page 86)

Challenge

Ana and Eric have a problem. Mrs. Blake helps them solve their problem. Complete the sentences below to tell what Ana, Eric, and Mrs. Blake are saying.

1.

Eric _____

_____

Well _____

_____

2.

Ana _____

_____

No _____

_____

3.

Mrs. Blake _____

_____

Yes _____

_____

Writing Application: An Interview

INFORMING

You are the host of a TV talk show. You are interviewing two scientists who have made an important discovery. Write the questions you ask the scientists and the answers that they give you. Begin each sentence with *yes, no, well,* or a scientist's name.

Name _____

7 Quotation Marks

> "Do you know anything about bears?" asked Meg.
> Leah said that bears were her favorite animals at the zoo.

Write these sentences correctly, adding quotation marks where they are needed. Write *correct* for each sentence that does not need quotation marks.

1. I know some interesting facts about polar bears, Leah said.

_____

2. Meg asked Leah which bears are the best hunters.

_____

3. Polar bears are the best hunters and swimmers, Leah answered.

_____

4. She added, Webbed front feet help them paddle in water.

_____

5. Polar bears are so beautiful! exclaimed Meg.

_____

6. Meg asked, How do polar bears stay warm in a cold climate?

_____

7. Leah replied, They have a thick layer of fat under their skin.

_____

8. Leah added that each hair in a polar bear's coat is hollow.

_____

9. The hollow hairs help the bear stay warm, said Leah.

_____

10. Meg exclaimed, What an interesting fact that is!

_____

(continued)

© Houghton Mifflin Harcourt Publishing Company

Grade 4: Unit 5 Capitalization and Punctuation *(Use with pupil book pages 182–183.)*
Skill: Students will use quotation marks in direct quotations.

7 Quotation Marks (continued from page 88)

Challenge

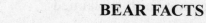

You are a scientist studying American black bears. Each day you watch the bears in the woods. At night you write notes about what you have seen, and you discuss what you have learned with other scientists. Here is a list of facts you have discovered about black bears.

BEAR FACTS

1. Black bears usually weigh up to three hundred pounds and are about five feet long.
2. Black bears climb trees when they are in danger.
3. They hardly ever leave the forest.
4. Black bears spend the winter in a den.
5. A cave or a hole in a fallen tree serves as a den.
6. Bear cubs are born in the den during the winter.

Now finish this conversation between you and the other scientists. Include some of the facts from your list.

Dr. B. Ware said, _____.

_____? asked Ms. Furr.

Mr. Griz Lee replied, _____.

I asked, _____?

_____, Ms. Furr answered.

Dr. B. Ware exclaimed, _____!

_____ , said Mr. Griz Lee.

I added, _____.

Writing Application: A Story

Write six sentences with quotations to finish this story: Bruno and Matilda were brown bears. One day they walked and walked. Suddenly they stepped out of the woods and into the parking lot of a giant mall. Bruno exclaimed, . . .

Grade 4: Unit 5 Capitalization and Punctuation *(Use with pupil book pages 182–183.)*
 Skill: Students will use quotation marks in direct quotations.

WORKBOOK PLUS
TCAP PRACTICE

89

Name _____

8 Quotations

Statement	"I have gone up in a balloon," Faith said.
Question	Dom asked, "What is it like to go up in a balloon?"
Command	Pia said, "Tell us about it."
Exclamation	"I can't wait to hear!" Dom exclaimed.

A These sentences have quotations. Write each sentence correctly.

1. ballooning is such an adventure Faith exclaimed

_____

2. tell me how the balloon works said Pia

_____

3. Pia asked do people race balloons

_____

4. Dom exclaimed I think balloon racing would be great

_____

B 5–12. This part of a story based on a historical event has eight errors in punctuation and capitalization. Use proofreading marks to correct the story.

Proofreading Marks

¶ Indent
∧ Add
ℰ Delete
≡ Capital letter
/ Small letter

Proofreading

The True Story of Three Farm Animals

In 1783, two French brothers sent a duck,

a rooster, and a sheep up in a hot-air balloon.

"Are we in a giant canopy bed? asked the sheep."

"What are those flames cried the duck.

"we're flying" cried the sheep.

The rooster said "we must be on a special mission from King

Louis XVI. We are teaching humans to fly."

(continued)

Grade 4: Unit 5 Capitalization and Punctuation *(Use with pupil book pages 184–185.)*
Skill: Students will capitalize and will punctuate direct quotations.

Name _____

8 Quotations (continued from page 90)

Challenge

Boris and Bertha are two hot-air balloons who have just escaped for an adventure of their own. Write a conversation between Boris and Bertha as they float across the countryside. Use a quotation in each sentence.

1. _____
2. _____
3. _____
4. _____
5. _____
6. _____

Writing Application: A Dialogue

You are riding in a balloon with a friend. You don't know exactly where you are. Write a conversation between you and your friend. Use a quotation in each sentence.

Grade 4: Unit 5 Capitalization and Punctuation (Use with pupil book pages 184–185.)

Skill: Students will capitalize and will punctuate direct quotations.

Name ____________________

9 Titles

Book: Adam of the Road **Magazine:** Time **Newspaper:** The City Journal

A Each sentence has a title in it. Write each sentence correctly.

1. Did you see the headline in today's pennsylvania gazette?

   ____

2. Carol liked the book called the phantom tollbooth.

   ____

3. I loved the pictures in the magazine animal kingdom.

   ____

4. Grandma read the wind in the willows to me.

   ____

5. Her picture appeared in yesterday's greenville globe.

   ____

6. Was charlie and the great glass elevator a funny book?

   ____

B 7–12. These wish lists have six incorrect titles. Use proofreading marks to correct the titles.

Example: Daniel's favorite book is the three Musketeers.

Proofreading Marks

- ¶ Indent
- ∧ Add
- Delete
- ≡ Capital letter
- / Small letter

Proofreading

My Reading Wish List

George's marvelous medicine

Julie of the wolves

subscription to Cricket

Mom's List

the philosophy of Immanuel Kant

365 Ways to Cook Chicken

Charles Kuralt's America

(continued)

Grade 4: Unit 5 Capitalization and Punctuation *(Use with pupil book pages 186–187.)*
Skill: Students will write titles of books, magazines, and newspapers correctly.

9 Titles (continued from page 92)

Challenge

Think about two books you have read that have become your favorites. Suppose that your teacher has displayed the two books on a shelf in your classroom. Your job is to make up a radio script as if the two books were talking to each other about themselves. In your script, be sure to capitalize titles of the books, as well as any titles your characters may have. Mention other book titles with which your books are comparing themselves. If you like, use humor in the book chat to keep your listeners tuned to the radio.

_____

_____

_____

_____

On another piece of paper, draw a picture of your school library or media center as the radio studio. Include the two books talking to each other. Decorate their titles.

Writing Application: A List

EXPRESSING

Write a list of your favorite things. Include books, movies, places, and things you own. Remember to capitalize the titles of some things.

Grade 4: Unit 5 Capitalization and Punctuation *(Use with pupil book pages 186–187.)*
  Skill: Students will use titles correctly.

**WORKBOOK PLUS
TCAP PRACTICE**   **93**

Name _____

1 What Is a Pronoun?

Nouns	Pronouns
<u>Lynn</u> wants to help.	**She** wants to help.
Matt cleans the <u>parks and streets</u>.	Matt cleans **them**.

Write the pronouns in these sentences. Then write the underlined words that they replace.

1. "Let us think of a way to clean up litter," said <u>Matt and Lynn</u>.

   _____

2. Lynn told <u>Matt</u> that he could use things over again.

   _____

3. <u>Dora and Ahmed</u> collected bottles. Matt wanted to help them.

   _____

4. <u>Lynn</u> wanted to help too. She had an idea.

   _____

5. "I have saved <u>newspapers</u>," said <u>Lynn</u>. Lynn wanted to recycle them.

   _____

6. "You must take out the papers," Lynn told <u>Matt</u>. "Help me," <u>Lynn</u> said.

   _____

7. <u>A truck</u> took the newspapers away. It came once a month.

   _____

8. "Now we should clean up the park," said <u>Matt and Lynn</u>.

   _____

9. <u>Matt</u> began to pick up paper from the grass. Lynn helped him.

   _____

10. At last <u>Matt and Lynn</u> finished working. They were happy and tired.

    _____

(continued)

Grade 4: Unit 6 Pronouns *(Use with pupil book pages 204–205.)*
Skill: Students will identify subject and object pronouns and the nouns
that they replace.

1 What Is a Pronoun? *(continued from page 94)*

Challenge

Here are four signs about cleaning up litter. Each sign is missing a pronoun. Write the correct pronouns on the signs.

TRASH!

Please put _____ in the right place.

OLD PAPERS?

Bring _____ to the Go-Round-Again store.

CLEAN UP!

Make the park sparkle for _____ all.

Riva Redo knows what to do. _____ returns bottles.

On another piece of paper, draw two signs about cleaning up litter. On each sign, write a sentence that uses a pronoun.

Writing Application: A Speech

EXPLAINING

You are running for mayor in your town or city. You have an idea for solving the town's litter problem. Write a speech about your idea. Use at least five pronouns in your speech.

Grade 4: Unit 6   Pronouns   *(Use with pupil book pages 204–205.)*
Skill: Students will use subject and object pronouns correctly.

WORKBOOK PLUS
TCAP PRACTICE

95

Name _____

2 Subject Pronouns

Nouns	Pronouns
Simon plays in the band.	He plays in the band.
Rachel is in the band too.	She is in the band too.
Simon and Rachel help each other.	They help each other.
The band is fun.	It is fun.

A Write the subject pronoun in each sentence.

1. We play in the music room every day
   after school.   _____

2. I play the trumpet in the band.   _____

3. It is a wonderful instrument.   _____

4. Have you ever played in a band?   _____

5. Next week Rachel and I will play at a town dance. _____

6. She was asked to play by Mr. Chu.   _____

7. He and Mrs. Russo had heard the band at a
   football game.   _____

8. They will be glad to hear the band play again.   _____

B Write each sentence. Use a subject pronoun in place of the
underlined word or words.

9. <u>Musicians</u> must learn to play the right notes.

   _____

10. <u>George</u> can play very high notes on the flute.

    _____

11. <u>Rachel</u> has learned to play the drums.

    _____

12. <u>Rachel and I</u> keep the beat for the band.

    _____

(continued)

Name _____

3 Object Pronouns (continued from page 98)

Challenge

Look at the pictures below. They show four steps in writing and publishing a book.

1.

3.

2.

4.

These four sentences tell about the pictures above. Write each sentence under the picture that it describes. Use an object pronoun in place of the underlined word or words.

> The editor thanks <u>Rita</u> for the book.
> The books are printed by <u>a printer</u>.
> Rita Lott writes <u>a book</u>.
> The editor corrects <u>the mistakes</u>.

Writing Application: A Report

Think of a job or a project that you have worked on with your friends or your family. Write a short description of this project. Use six object pronouns.

© Houghton Mifflin Harcourt Publishing Company

Grade 4: Unit 6 Pronouns *(Use with pupil book pages 208–209.)*
Skill: Students will use object pronouns correctly.

WORKBOOK PLUS
TCAP PRACTICE

99

Writing with Pronouns

Unclear pronoun	Mr. Norris smiled as Jeremy entered the elevator. He pressed the button to close the door.
Pronoun replaced with a noun	Mr. Norris smiled as Jeremy entered the elevator. **Mr. Norris** pressed the button to close the door.

Writing Clearly with Pronouns 1–5. Rewrite the sentences within this story that have underlined pronouns. Replace the underlined pronouns with nouns.

> **Revising**
>
> Jenny Mouse lives in the country. One day, Jenny traveled to the city to visit her cousin, Annie Mouse. Annie took Jenny to the tallest building in town. <u>She</u> had never seen anything like it. From the observation deck on the top floor, Annie and Jenny looked at the buildings and cars below. It seemed that <u>they</u> could see for miles. Annie put a coin in the telescope. Then she pointed <u>it</u> at an apartment building across from a park. "I live over there," she told her cousin. Annie flitted from one window to another, trying to see everything, but the view made Jenny dizzy. <u>She</u> couldn't wait to get back on solid ground again.
>
> The next day <u>she</u> went to the train station with Jenny.
>
> "Come again soon!" called Annie, as the train pulled out of the station.

1. _____

_____

2. _____

_____

3. _____

_____

4. _____

_____

5. _____

_____

(continued)

Name _____

1 What Is an Adverb?

How	Jake **quickly** threw the ball. I ran **fast**.
When	**Finally**, I caught the ball. **Then** I felt a pain in my foot.
Where	**Down** I fell. Jake helped me **inside**.

A Write each adverb. Label it *how, when,* or *where.*

1. My foot hurt badly. _____

2. My mother quickly called the doctor. _____

3. Soon Dr. Kay answered the phone. _____

4. He works downtown. _____

5. Mother drove me there. _____

6. A nurse helped me inside. _____

7. Then she brought me a wheelchair. _____

8. We rode the elevator up. _____

9. Later, the nurse took my temperature. _____

10. Dr. Kay examined me carefully. _____

B Underline each adverb. Write the verb it describes.

11. Dr. Kay often asks important questions. _____

12. He always listens to my heart. _____

13. I breathed slowly for him. _____

14. He moved my sore foot gently. _____

15. Dr. Kay finally took a picture of my foot. _____

16. The picture clearly showed a broken bone. _____

17. He skillfully made a new cast for my foot. _____

18. I walked out on a pair of crutches. _____

(continued)

Grade 4: Unit 7 Adverbs and Prepositions *(Use with pupil book pages 234–235.)*
Skill: Students will identify adverbs and the verbs that they modify.

WORKBOOK PLUS TCAP PRACTICE 111

Name _____

1 What Is an Adverb? (continued from page 111)

Challenge

Tom Swift is a character in a book who always speaks in a special way. Read the two examples of Tom's sentences. Notice that the way Tom says something always matches an idea in the sentence. Now complete Tom's sentences below, using the adverbs from the Word Box.

Examples: "I'm <u>not nervous</u>," Tom said **calmly.**

Tom said **smartly**, "I got <u>the highest grade</u> on the test."

sourly	clumsily	firmly	rapidly	pointedly
brightly	coldly	stiffly	sharply	patiently

1. "Turn on the light," Tom said _____.

2. "Please hand me my coat and gloves," Tom said _____.

3. "You are going much too fast," Tom replied _____.

4. "These scissors will cut anything," Tom announced _____.

5. Tom said _____, "You're squeezing my arm."

6. "I'm going to see the doctor," Tom said _____.

7. "Will you sharpen my pencil?" Tom asked _____.

8. Tom said _____, "Don't trip over the bucket."

9. "I have to iron a shirt," Tom said _____.

10. "Are pickles your favorite snack?" Tom asked _____.

On another piece of paper, write three more sentences that Tom might say.

Writing Application: Instructions

You are a doctor, and one of your patients has asked for instructions on staying healthy. Write six sentences that tell your patient how to stay healthy. Use an adverb in each sentence.

Grade 4: Unit 7 Adverbs and Prepositions (Use with pupil book pages 234–235.)
Skill: Students will use adverbs in sentences.

Name _____

Writing with Adverbs

Brad displayed his coin collection at a hobby show.
Brad **eagerly** displayed his coin collection at a hobby show.
Eagerly, Brad displayed his coin collection at a hobby show.
Brad displayed his coin collection **eagerly** at a hobby show.

Elaborating Sentences 1–8. Rewrite this paragraph from a school newspaper. Elaborate each sentence with an adverb. Use the adverbs in the box or choose your own.

yesterday	proudly	neatly	now
always	before	finally	carefully

Revising

My brother Pete wanted to be a collector. He had started many collections, but he lost interest. He has found something that is exciting. He collects sand from different places. Pete pours each bag of sand into a glass jar. He labels each bottle with the place where the sand was found. He shows his collection to anyone who is interested. He showed me his newest addition, which is black sand from Italy.

_____

_____

_____

_____

_____

_____

_____

_____

_____

_____

(continued)

Grade 4: Unit 7 Adverbs and Prepositions *(Use with pupil book pages 236–237.)*
  Skill: Students will elaborate sentences with adverbs.

Name _____

Writing with Adverbs (continued from page 113)

Two sentences	My friends and I ride our bikes. We ride often.
Combined sentence	My friends and I **often** ride our bikes.

Combining Sentences 9–14. Rewrite the diary entry. Combine each pair of related sentences by moving an adverb from the second sentence to the first.

Revising

I fell off my bike. I fell off it today. Dad called the doctor. He called quickly. The doctor said, "Come over to my office." He said, "Come now."

Dr. Ben examined me. He examined me carefully. My foot is bruised but not broken. It is badly bruised. I limped out of the office. I limped slowly.

_____

_____

_____

_____

_____

_____

_____

_____

Grade 4: Unit 7 Adverbs and Prepositions *(Use with pupil book pages 236–237.)*
Skill: Students will combine sentences by moving an adverb.

Name _____

2 Comparing with Adverbs

Adverb	Comparing Two Actions	Comparing Three or More
fast	fast**er**	fast**est**
quietly	**more** quietly	**most** quietly
Incorrect		Correct
We stayed <u>more later</u> than he did.		We stayed **later** than he did.
They played <u>quietliest</u> of all.		They played **most quietly** of all.

A Write each sentence. Use the correct form of the adverb in parentheses.

1. Roberto arrived at the park _____ than we did. **(soon)**

    _____

2. We waited _____ than he did for the concert to begin. **(patiently)**

    _____

3. Of all our group, Fran sat _____ to the bandstand. **(near)**

    _____

4. She watched the musicians _____ than we did. **(closely)**

    _____

5. We cheered _____ of all for "The Stars and Stripes Forever." **(eagerly)**

    _____

B 6–10. Use proofreading marks to correct the five incorrect adverb forms in this description for an article.

Example: We listened ~~careful~~ ᴄᴀʀᴇꜰᴜʟʟʏ as the band played.

Proofreading

The band has to play loud than the noisy crowd. The

flutes play softlier than the horns. The boom of the drum

sounds most loudest of all. We hear it soonest than the horns.

That boom travels quickliest to our ears!

Proofreading Marks	
¶	Indent
∧	Add
℘	Delete
≡	Capital letter
/	Small letter

(continued)

Grade 4: Unit 7   Adverbs and Prepositions *(Use with pupil book pages 238–239.)*
Skill: Students will write the comparative and the superlative forms
    of adverbs.

**WORKBOOK PLUS
TCAP PRACTICE**

115

Name _____

2 Comparing with Adverbs (continued from page 115)

Challenge

John Philip Sousa invented a new kind of tuba called the sousaphone. The musicians in the pictures below have invented their own instruments too. Make up a name for each instrument, using the inventor's name.

  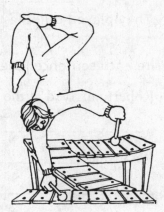

Chuck Flutie   **Curlie Moppet**   **Craig Z. Keys**

_____   _____   _____

Now invent an instrument that is named after you. Write its name and a short description of the instrument.

_____

_____

You and the musicians shown above have given a concert together. On another piece of paper, write a short review of this concert. Use adverbs to compare the way you and the other musicians played your instruments, moved on stage, dressed, and performed.

COMPARING AND CONTRASTING

Writing Application: An Advertisement

Suppose that you are a member of a band. Write an advertisement for your band's next show. Give the band a name. Then write five sentences for the advertisement. Use adverbs to compare your band's playing and performance with those of other bands in your town.

© Houghton Mifflin Harcourt Publishing Company

116 **WORKBOOK PLUS**
TCAP PRACTICE

Grade 4: Unit 7   Adverbs and Prepositions   (Use with pupil book pages 238–239.)
Skill: Students will use the comparative and the superlative forms of adverbs.

Name _____

3 Using *good* and *well*

Adjective	Adverb
We saw a **good** rodeo.	The riders performed **well**.
This seat is **good**.	Can you see the riders **well**?

A Write *good* or *well* to complete each sentence correctly.

1. A _____ rodeo was held on July 4, 1892.

2. That rodeo gave Buffalo Bill Cody a _____ idea.

3. He performed _____ in many rodeo events.

4. People enjoyed watching _____ riders.

5. Buffalo Bill thought a traveling show might do _____.

6. It would be _____ to combine a rodeo and a circus.

B 7–12. Use proofreading marks to correct six mistakes in the use of *good* and *well* in this review of a school play.

Example: The clowns did ~~good~~ *well* at making people laugh.

Proofreading Marks

¶	Indent
∧	Add
⌿	Delete
≡	Capital letter
/	Small letter

Proofreading

REVIEW

Last night, the Rodeo Middle School performed very

good in the Wild West Show. Ray Vieira played Buffalo Bill Cody. He did

a well job of playing a cowboy, and he spoke good as the host of the show.

Sandra Melendez played Annie Oakley good, even though she kept dropping

her water pistol on the stage. One star of the show, Wild Bill Hickok, was

very well, and his costume disguised him so good that it was a surprise

to find out he was my real-life brother! Everyone had a good time.

(continued)

Grade 4: Unit 7 Adverbs and Prepositions *(Use with pupil book pages 240–241.)*
Skill: Students will use *good* and *well* correctly.

**WORKBOOK PLUS
TCAP PRACTICE** 117

Name _____

3 Using *good* and *well* (continued from page 117)

Challenge

Buffalo Bill's Wild West Circus had many exciting performers. The posters below show performers who might have appeared in the Wild West Circus. Complete the sentence about each performer. Use the word *good* or *well* in each sentence.

1. Jumping Jane _____

_____

2. Lasso Luke _____

_____

3. Juggling Jethro _____

_____

Now name two more performers who might have appeared in the Wild West Circus. Write a sentence about each performer, using the word *good* or *well*. On another piece of paper, design a poster advertising one performer's act.

4. _____

5. _____

Writing Application: A News Article

You are a newspaper reporter. Write a short news article about a rodeo, a circus, or another traveling show that has come to your town. Describe your favorite performers and their acts. Use the word *good* or *well* in each sentence.

4 Negatives

Michelle had **never** been to a museum before. **No one** had ever taken her.	
Incorrect	She **hadn't** gone **nowhere** like that.
Correct	She **hadn't** gone **anywhere** like that. She **had** gone **nowhere** like that.

A Underline the correct word in parentheses to complete each sentence.

1. Michelle hadn't been to (no, any) art museums.

2. She couldn't find (anyone, no one) to take her.

3. Didn't (anybody, nobody) like art as much as she did?

4. Michelle (had, hadn't) no choice but to go by herself.

5. This museum didn't have (nothing, anything) painted by Picasso.

6. Michelle (hasn't, has) never seen one of Picasso's paintings.

B 7–10. Use proofreading marks to correct four mistakes in the use of negatives in this poem.

Example: Our museum ~~hasn't~~ ^has^ nothing but sculptures.

Proofreading

Proofreading Marks

¶	Indent
∧	Add
⌐	Delete
≡	Capital letter
/	Small letter

I haven't seen no paintings by Grandma Moses.

I don't know Monet's lilies from any roses,

But I do know that I wouldn't like nothing better

Than to visit an art museum.

I'd go when there wasn't no one else there,

Then no one wouldn't tell me not to stare,

And I'd go up and down on the escalator,

And the art works? Of course, I'd see 'em.

(continued)

Grade 4: Unit 7 Adverbs and Prepositions *(Use with pupil book pages 242–243.)*
  Skill: Students will use negatives correctly.

WORKBOOK PLUS
TCAP PRACTICE   119

Name _____

4 Negatives (continued from page 119)

Challenge

Find the word from the Word Box that completes each sentence. Then use your answers to complete the crossword puzzle.

anywhere	none	never	any	anything	nothing
anybody	no	nowhere	ever	anyone	nobody

ACROSS

3. I had __?__ visited the new museum.

4. I hadn't seen __?__ of its exhibits before.

5. In the museum, we didn't go __?__ alone.

7. There were __?__ other groups visiting.

9. Didn't __?__ see the Crazy Puzzle?

DOWN

1. Have you __?__ seen the Shirt Room?

2. It didn't have __?__ but unusual shirts.

6. __?__ wanted to leave so soon.

8. Hasn't __?__ read the museum books?

10. I have read __?__ of them so far.

Writing Application: A Letter

Think of a museum or a historic building that you have visited. Remember what you liked and disliked about your visit. Write a letter to the director, politely suggesting ways to improve the exhibits and programs. Use negatives correctly.

Grade 4: Unit 7 Adverbs and Prepositions (Use with pupil book pages 242–243.)
Skill: Students will use negatives correctly.

5 What Is a Preposition?

Common Prepositions						
about	around	beside	for	near	outside	under
above	at	by	from	of	over	until
across	before	down	in	off	past	up
after	behind	during	inside	on	through	with
along	below	except	into	out	to	without

Write each sentence below. Underline the prepositional phrase once and the preposition twice.

1. This morning I was wide awake before sunrise.

   _____

2. I had heard a loud sound in the driveway.

   _____

3. Two men were unloading a huge crate from a delivery truck.

   _____

4. Suddenly, a crate flew open and fell to the ground.

   _____

5. There was definitely something alive inside the crate!

   _____

6. Just then I heard Dad calling me, and I raced down the stairs.

   _____

7. Dad asked, "Have you been e-shopping without my permission?"

   _____

8. I suddenly remembered what I did last Monday after school.

   _____

9. I ran outside and peered into the crate.

   _____

10. The lion cub that I had ordered was hiding under some straw.

   _____

(continued)

Grade 4: Unit 7 Adverbs and Prepositions *(Use with pupil book pages 244–245.)*
Skill: Students will identify prepositions and prepositional phrases.

WORKBOOK PLUS
TCAP PRACTICE   121

Name _____

5 What Is a Preposition? (continued from page 121)

Challenge

Look at the picture and write a preposition to complete each sentence.

1. A milk carton is _____ the top shelf.

2. Bottles and cans fit _____ the refrigerator door.

3. Two bins _____ the shelves keep fruits and vegetables crisp.

4. The butter dish is _____ the bottles and cans.

5. Some pears are _____ the cheese.

6. The jar _____ mayonnaise is new.

7. The juice is _____ the milk.

8. Erin made dinner _____ the whole family.

9. We will have chicken _____ a cream sauce.

10. Who scraped the frosting _____ the cake?

Writing Application: A Recipe

Write instructions for a favorite recipe. Use at least five prepositional phrases in your instructions.

© Houghton Mifflin Harcourt Publishing Company

Grade 4: Unit 7   Adverbs and Prepositions   (Use with pupil book pages 244–245.)
Skill: Students will write prepositions.

Name _____

Writing with Prepositions

Without prepositional phrase	Rabbits nibble grass.
With prepositional phrase	Rabbits nibble grass **in the meadow**.

Elaborating Sentences 1–8. Rewrite the paragraph. Elaborate each sentence with a prepositional phrase from the box, or create your own.

into a huge pile	for the ducks	about the warm weather
under the trees	after lunch	in the morning
through the park	with the long neck	to the swan

Revising

Everyone was excited. We played outdoors. We rode our bikes. Mom brought a bag of corn and birdseed. The beautiful white swan swam toward us. I threw some of the corn. We watched the squirrels scamper. We raked our leaves and jumped in them.

_____

_____

_____

_____

_____

_____

_____

_____

(continued)

Grade 4: Unit 7   Adverbs and Prepositions   *(Use with pupil book pages 246–247.)*
   Skill: Students will elaborate sentences by adding prepositional phrases.

Name _____

Writing with Prepositions (continued from page 123)

Two sentences	The skaters glide gracefully.
	They glide over the ice.
Combined sentence	The skaters glide gracefully **over the ice**.

Combining Sentences 9–14. Rewrite this segment from a review of an ice skating competition. Combine each pair of related sentences by adding the underlined prepositional phrase from one sentence to the sentence before it.

Revising

Gina skated confidently. She skated onto the rink. Her colorful costume sparkled. It sparkled in the lights. Beautiful music echoed loudly. It echoed throughout the arena. She performed magnificent spins and jumps. She performed them for the audience. The audience clapped loudly. The audience clapped after her performance. Gina waved happily. She waved to the cheering fans.

_____

_____

_____

_____

_____

_____

_____

_____

_____

Grade 4: Unit 7 Adverbs and Prepositions (Use with pupil book page 247.)
Skill: Students will combine sentences by moving a prepositional phrase.

Name _____

Changing Meaning with Adverbs

> The crowd cheered **loudly**.
> The crowd cheered **politely**.

early	nervously	finally
happily	patiently	skillfully
wildly	carefully	clumsily
late	well	noisily
sadly	anxiously	confidently

1-10. Write this paragraph. Fill in the blanks with adverbs from the box. Then compare your paragraph with one written by a classmate. Notice the difference in meaning created by using different adverbs.

Revising

It was a big day for the Spartans. The team had been waiting _____ for the championship game to begin. The players gathered _____ around their coach. They listened _____ to his instructions. _____, it was time for the team to take the floor. The crowd cheered _____ for the home team. _____ in the game, the score was tied. Both teams played _____. With three seconds left, Jim _____ shot the basketball. The Spartans left the court _____. They knew that they had played _____.

_____

_____

_____

_____

_____

_____

_____

_____

Grade 4: Unit 7 Adverbs and Prepositions *(Use with pupil book page 248.)*
Skill: Students will use different adverbs to change the meaning of a paragraph.

Name _____

Supporting Sentences

A paragraph that tells a story is a **narrative paragraph.** It often has a lead sentence, supporting sentences, and a concluding sentence. **Supporting sentences** support the main idea by giving details about it. They answer one or more of these questions: *Who? What? Where? When? Why? How?*

Complete the narrative paragraph about this picture. Read the lead sentence below. Next, find details in the picture to support the main idea in the lead sentence. Then write three supporting sentences, using the details.

Yesterday was such a great day that I was determined to play every game.

_____

_____

_____

_____

_____

_____

_____

_____

_____

_____

I was worn out, but I sure had fun!

126 **WORKBOOK PLUS**
TCAP PRACTICE   **Grade 4:** Section 1 Narrating and Entertaining *(Use with pupil book pages 269–273.)*
Skill: Students will complete a narrative paragraph with supporting sentences.

Organizing Your Narrative

	The Day the Dishwasher Overflowed
2	suds and water everywhere
1	put in the soap and turned it on
	~~got a pet hamster that day~~
3	plumber made an emergency stop

Three events for a personal narrative are underlined below. Number each event 1, 2, or 3 to show the order in which it happened. Cross out details that do not keep to the topic. Then organize the main events and supporting details in the chart below.

Topic: summer sledding at Canyon Lake

Event ____

sledding in box

climb up sand dune

Kim slides down in box.

Tomorrow I want to swim.

I try it!

Event ____

planning sledding trip

middle of summer

Kim is my favorite cousin.

need snow to sled

Kim says, "You'll see."

Event ____

arriving at Canyon Lake

high sand dunes around lake

stopped in town for gas

Kim's big box

hike to dunes

Topic	Main Events	Details
	1.	
	2.	
	3.	

Grade 4: Unit 8 Personal Narrative *(Use with pupil book page 284.)*
  Skill: Students will arrange main events in story order and choose supporting details that describe each event.

WORKBOOK PLUS
TCAP PRACTICE

127

Good Beginnings

Weak Beginning	Strong Beginnings		
I walk my dog bright and early every morning.	**Question**	**Surprising Statement**	**Dialogue**
	What gets you out of bed faster than an alarm clock?	In the early morning, I often wonder whether I walk my dog or he walks me.	"Wait! Just let me tie my shoelaces!" I pleaded.

Each short narrative below needs a beginning. First, read the story. Then write a strong beginning, using the strategy suggested.

1. . . . Then I closed my eyes and concentrated really hard. I started to picture myself standing in the middle of a tropical forest surrounded by strange animals. However, it was just my dad, a would-be opera singer, singing in the shower.

   Question: _____

   _____

   _____

   _____

2. . . . I planted the "wonder seeds" that I had ordered. The flowers that grew were huge, and the tomato plants filled the back porch. I grew enough tomatoes to make spaghetti sauce for the entire neighborhood!

   Surprising Statement: _____

   _____

   _____

   _____

3. . . . I followed her into her room. She opened a small box and took out a black pearl ring. She said, "I wore this ring when I was your age. If it fits your finger, it will bring you good luck." It fit perfectly!

   Dialogue: _____

   _____

   _____

   _____

Grade 4: Unit 8 Personal Narrative *(Use with pupil book page 285.)*
Skill: Students will write strong beginnings for personal narratives, using three different strategies.

Name _____

Writing with Voice

Weak Voice	Strong Voice
I liked school this year. Our class was putting on a play. Mr. Gee asked me if I wanted to be on the stage crew. I said I did. I moved scenery and worked the curtain.	This was my best school year ever. I had a big role in the class play, but it wasn't on-stage. When Mr. Gee asked me if I wanted to be part of the stage crew, I said, "Sign me up!" With all the cool scenery and props to get ready, I had as much fun backstage as I would have had on the stage.

The story below is dull and boring. It sounds flat. Rewrite the narrative to give it a stronger voice. Make the story your own by writing it so that it sounds like you. Let your personality shine through.

    Last summer, my best friend and I decided to sell lemonade. It was easy. We went to the basketball courts near our house. That was where the boys in high school played ball. We knew that they would be thirsty. We had two pitchers of lemonade and a lot of paper cups. The basketball players bought all of the lemonade. We ran out of lemonade and made fourteen dollars.

_____
_____
_____
_____
_____
_____
_____
_____
_____
_____
_____
_____

Name _____

Good Endings

Weak Ending	Strong Ending
My team beat the best girl's soccer team in our league.	I couldn't believe what happened. We trounced the best girl's soccer team in our league and broke our losing streak in one afternoon! What a victory that was!

Each short narrative below needs an ending. First, read the story. Then write two endings for it. Read your story endings and decide which one is stronger. Put a check mark in front of the stronger ending.

1.   At first I didn't want to spend Saturday afternoon with Aunt Gina. I thought I would be bored, but that changed the minute I walked in the door. First, we baked brownies and made apple crisp. Then we went to a yard sale and had a contest to see who could find the most useless thing to buy. I won when I pulled one green and purple sock out of a pile of clothes. My prize was a trip to the movies.

Ending: _____

_____

_____

Ending: _____

_____

_____

2.   The ocean was just too big and deep. I did not want to go swimming. Then I tickled my toes along the shore. The water was warm enough, so I waded in a short way. I felt something under my foot. It was a clam shell. Then I spotted something white and horn-shaped. It was a snail shell. The ocean was turning out to be a fascinating place.

Ending: _____

_____

_____

Ending: _____

_____

_____

Grade 4: Unit 8 Personal Narrative (Use with pupil book page 287.)
Skill: Students will write two endings for each narrative and then choose the stronger ending.

Revising a Personal Narrative

Have I	yes
• written a new beginning that will grab my readers' attention?	❑
• given the writing my own voice?	❑
• added details to help readers see, hear, and feel the experience?	❑
• told the events in order?	❑
• revised the ending to make the story feel finished?	❑

Revise the following narrative to make it better. Use the checklist above to help you. Check off each box when you have finished your revision. You can use the spaces above the lines, on the sides, and below the paragraph for your changes.

The Day I Hit the Winning Home Run

It was my turn to bat. The bases were loaded. There were

two outs. I walked to the plate and held the bat. I waited for

the pitch. I missed the ball. The umpire called a strike. The

crowd groaned. I swung again. I heard the umpire say strike.

If I struck out, my team would lose. It would be my fault. The

pitcher was getting ready for her next pitch. I felt the bat hit

the ball. I ran as fast as I could, and I heard the crowd cheering

as my foot touched home plate. I had hit a home run. My team

had won the game!

© Houghton Mifflin Harcourt Publishing Company

Grade 4: Unit 8 Personal Narrative *(Use with pupil book page 288.)*
Skill: Students will revise a personal narrative, using a revision checklist.

WORKBOOK PLUS
TCAP PRACTICE **131**

Name _____

Elaborating: Details

Few details	Felisa cleaned off her desk.
Elaborated with details	Felisa put her pencils and her books in a drawer, lined up her toy frog collection on a shelf, and wiped her desktop clean. She even put her papers in a neat pile.

The following narrative is boring because it doesn't contain enough details. Revise the narrative, adding details to make it more interesting.

I read books to my little brother last summer. It was my job. At first it was boring. Then we both started to have fun. I liked finding good books. He laughed at the different voices I used too. It was fun to perform.

_____

_____

_____

_____

_____

_____

_____

_____

_____

_____

_____

_____

_____

Grade 4: Unit 8 Personal Narrative *(Use with pupil book page 290.)*
Skill: Students will revise a personal narrative, elaborating with interesting details.

Name _____

Planning Characters

When you plan your story **characters**, use details to help your readers get to know the characters inside and out. Think about what your characters look like, how they act, and what they say. Think about your characters' feelings and interests.

Think about the main character in a story you might write. Does the character wear a uniform? make people laugh? love computer games? Write details about the character on the lines in each category. Draw a picture of your character. Then write a sentence that describes your character's personality.

How my character looks

_____

_____

_____

How my character feels

_____

_____

_____

What my character is like

_____

_____

_____

How my character acts

_____

_____

_____

What my character says

_____

_____

_____

My character's interests

_____

_____

_____

_____

_____

_____

_____

Grade 4: Unit 9 Story *(Use with pupil book page 306.)*
Skill: Students will plan characters by listing details.

WORKBOOK PLUS
TCAP PRACTICE 133

Name _____

Planning Setting and Plot

The **setting** for a story is when and where it takes place. The **plot** focuses on the main problem in the story and has three parts—a beginning, a middle, and an end. The **beginning** of a story introduces the characters, the setting, and the problem. The **middle** tells how the characters deal with the problem. The **end** of a story explains how the problem is solved.

Think about a story you know well. Make a story map that shows the beginning, the middle, and the end of the story. Include notes about the characters, the setting, and the problem.

Beginning
introduces the main characters, setting, and problem

_____
_____
_____

Middle
tells how the characters deal with the problem

End
explains how the problem is solved

_____
_____

© Houghton Mifflin Harcourt Publishing Company

Grade 4: Unit 9   Story   *(Use with pupil book page 307.)*
Skill: Students will complete a story map showing the three main parts of a plot—beginning, middle, and end.

Name _____

Developing Characters

Telling	Showing
Billy's brother came home from the movie and told Billy all about it.	Billy's older brother ran all the way home from the movie, rushed in the door, and immediately started acting out all the characters' parts for Billy.

Telling, Without Dialogue	Showing, with Dialogue
Abe can't stop talking about his new bike.	"Wait until you see my new bike!" exclaimed Abe. "It is so cool! I feel as though I'm flying when I ride it. I'd better be careful, though, or I'll get a speeding ticket!"

Rewrite the story below by adding dialogue to show what the characters are like. Remember that you can show your characters' thoughts, feelings, and personalities by what they say.

Rosemary gently lifted her caramel-colored kitten out of its basket. She lovingly carried it into the kitchen, where her mother was working. Rosemary had been struggling to think of a name for her adorable new pet. She hoped that her mother might have an idea. Rosemary's mom was very creative. Rosemary knew she could count on Mom for the perfect name.

_____
_____
_____
_____
_____
_____
_____
_____
_____

Grade 4: Unit 9 Story *(Use with pupil book page 308.)*
Skill: Students will revise a story by adding characters' dialogue.

WORKBOOK PLUS
TCAP PRACTICE 135

Name _____

Developing the Plot

Good Beginnings	
Describe the setting	The waves crashed against the rugged rocks on the shore as the spindly trees twisted in the wind.
Describe a character	The crowd gasped as Trina glided onto the ice in her glittering sequined costume and her sparkling silver tiara.
Describe an action	The boys carefully positioned themselves on the toboggan, pushed off, and whizzed down the hill at breakneck speed!

The story below needs a good beginning. Write two good beginnings. The strategies above will help you. Put a check by the beginning that you like better.

Elizabeth thought she would never be able to stay calm under such pressure. As she walked up the steps to the high dive, she thought, "I know I can do this. I know I can do this."

When she reached the end of the diving board, Elizabeth raised her hands over her head to get into position. She whispered to herself, "You've done a back dive hundreds of times. Just pretend you're doing it for the coach."

After the dive was completed and she hit the water, Elizabeth knew she had done a good job. She swam to the edge of the pool and looked up at her coach. "Way to go, Champ," he said. "That dive clinched first place."

My Beginning: _____

_____

_____

_____

My Beginning: _____

_____

_____

_____

136 WORKBOOK PLUS
TCAP PRACTICE

Grade 4: Unit 9 Story *(Use with pupil book pages 309–310.)*
Skill: Students will write good beginnings for a story.

Name _____

Writing with Voice

Weak Voice	Strong Voice
Billy opened his birthday present and smiled. It was what he wanted.	Billy tore open the wrapping on his birthday gift. When he saw what was inside, he could barely speak. The words came out garbled. He had thought no one knew his secret birthday wish.

The story below is dull and boring. It does not have a voice. Rewrite the story, using voice to let the audience know the characters' personalities. Use details to make the story sound the way you want it to. Then give the story a good ending.

The king called his three daughters together. He told them it was time to choose the one who would wear the crown. He explained that he would give the girls a test. Each daughter had to solve a puzzle. This would be a challenge.

The girls thought and thought. Each knew she would have to use her wits to win the crown.

Grade 4: Unit 9   Story   *(Use with pupil book page 311.)*
Skill: Students will revise a story, using voice.

WORKBOOK PLUS
TCAP PRACTICE   137

Name _____

Revising a Story

Have I   **yes**
- written a new beginning that grabs readers' attention and introduces the characters, the setting, and the problem? ❑
- added details and dialogue that make the story come alive? ❑
- given the characters a voice and made the story sound the way I want? ❑
- ended the story by telling how the problem works out? ❑

Revise the following story to make it better. Use the checklist above to help you. Check each box when you have finished your revision. You can use the spaces above the lines, on the sides, and below the paragraph for your changes.

Travel Adventure

Jason told his brother Ben that there was nothing left to discover in the world. He was sure that he had seen everything, at least in a book or on television. Ben said no way. So the two brothers set off on an adventure trip.

They saw a chameleon in Saudi Arabia and a cheetah in Sri Lanka. "I've seen those," said Jason, yawning.

The trip was almost over, and nothing had surprised Jason. The boys were sitting on a hillside in Ethiopia when Jason shouted, "What's that?" He was staring at a big, wild goat with huge, jagged horns. Ben told him that it was a Walia ibex.

Name _____

Elaborating: Details

Without details	Sandra ate an apple.
Elaborated with details	Sandra ate an apple in the kitchen with her sister.

The following story would be more interesting if it had more details. Revise the story by adding prepositional phrases to some of the sentences.

Sabrina never dreamed that she might be on a quiz show. Then the call came. The producers had called her school. Eliot knew a great deal. Ann was an expert. Sema was great too. But Sabrina was good at two things. She knew about American history and about musicals. Of course, the producers picked Sabrina.

_____

_____

_____

_____

_____

_____

_____

_____

_____

_____

_____

_____

Grade 4: Unit 9 Story *(Use with pupil book page 314.)*
Skill: Students will elaborate a story by adding prepositional phrases.

**WORKBOOK PLUS
TCAP PRACTICE** 139

Name _____

Supporting Sentences

> A paragraph that gives factual information is called an **informational paragraph**. It often has a topic sentence, supporting sentences, and a closing sentence. **Supporting sentences** give details that tell about the main idea of the paragraph. These details often include facts. They may also include sensory words that describe how things look, smell, feel, taste, and sound.

Complete the informational paragraph. Look at the diagram, and read the topic sentence and the closing sentence below. Then write at least three supporting sentences, using information from the diagram.

College Basketball Scoring

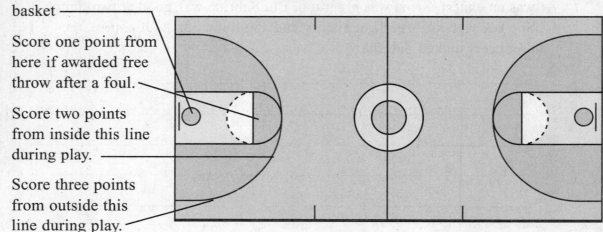

basket

Score one point from here if awarded free throw after a foul.

Score two points from inside this line during play.

Score three points from outside this line during play.

The only way to make points in basketball is to throw the ball into the basket.

_____

_____

_____

_____

_____

_____

_____

Where you are when you shoot makes an important difference to your score.

140   WORKBOOK PLUS
TCAP PRACTICE   Grade 4: Section 2   Explaining and Informing   *(Use with pupil book pp. 331–337.)*
                       Skill: Students will complete an informational paragraph with supporting sentences.

Organizing Your Instructions

Steps	Materials Needed	Details
1 First, arrange the chairs.	chairs (one per player, minus one)	
2 Now start the music.	music CD, CD player with remote control	

The pictures and steps below describe how to make sock puppets, but they are out of order. Number the steps to show the correct order. Then fill in the chart by writing the steps in order and listing materials that are needed.

_____ Next, glue on felt lips.

_____ Then glue on yarn for hair.

_____ Finally, when the glue has dried, put on a show!

_____ First, sew buttons on for eyes and nose.

Steps	Materials Needed	
1		
2		
3		
4		

Grade 4: Unit 10   Instructions   *(Use with pupil book page 349.)*
Skill: Students will organize instructions by putting steps in order.

WORKBOOK PLUS
TCAP PRACTICE

141

Name _____

Using Details

Without Exact Details	With Exact Details
Fold a piece of paper. Attach the pieces with string.	Fold a piece of paper in half, and then fold it again. Cut the squares apart, and punch a hole in the top of each. Next, string the squares together.

The Step-by-Step Chart below lists the steps and materials for making a mobile. Look at the picture, and add details to the chart. Then use the chart to help you write a set of instructions. Remember to include exact details.

Steps	Materials Needed	Details
1 First, make interesting paper shapes.	old newspaper and magazines, scissors, glue	
2 Next, attach bottles to hanger.	plastic bottles, shoelaces or used string, wire coat hanger	
3 When glue dries, attach shapes to hanger.	shapes from Step 1, more string, mobile	

_____

_____

_____

_____

_____

Name _____

Good Beginnings and Endings

Weak Beginning	Strong Beginning
You can make a box with art sticks.	Do you need a place to keep small personal objects?

Weak Ending	Strong Ending
Now your little box is ready to use.	It's small, it's private, and it's ready to use!

The instructional paragraph below needs a better beginning and a better ending. First, read the paragraph. Then replace the underlined sentences. Write two interesting beginnings and circle the one that you think is stronger. Then write two strong endings and circle the one that you like better.

Planting a flower garden is a good idea. You will need some seeds, a small shovel, and a plot with rich soil. First, read the instructions on the seed packet to find out how deeply you should dig. Then find a small area that gets enough sunlight. Now dig the holes and place the seeds in the ground. Next, cover them with dirt. Finally, drench the area with water. Be sure to water your plants regularly while they are growing. That's how you grow flowers.

Beginning: _____

_____

_____

Beginning: _____

_____

_____

Ending: _____

_____

_____

Ending: _____

_____

_____

Grade 4: Unit 10   Instructions   *(Use with pupil book page 351.)*
   Skill: Students will write strong beginnings and endings for instructions.

WORKBOOK PLUS
TCAP PRACTICE

143

Name _____

Revising Instructions

Have I   **yes**
- written a new beginning that states the topic in an interesting way? ❑
- included all the steps in the correct order? ❑
- listed all the materials needed for each step? ❑
- added clear, exact details for the steps? ❑
- revised the ending to wrap up the instructions? ❑

Revise the following instructional paragraph to make it better. Use the checklist above to help you. Check off each box when you have finished your revision. You can use the spaces above the lines, along the sides, and below the paragraph for your changes.

Puzzle Party Invitations

Here's how to make puzzle party invitations. Write each

invitation on a card or thick construction paper. Use pens.

Then cut each invitation into puzzle pieces. Put all the pieces

for each invitation into an envelope. Address the envelopes,

seal them, and put a stamp on each one. Finally, mail the

invitations.

Grade 4: Unit 10   Instructions   *(Use with pupil book page 352.)*
Skill: Students will revise a set of instructions, using a revision checklist.

Name _____

Sentence Fluency

Sentences all the same length	Find some clear plastic wrap. Cut off a large piece. Tape it to a mirror. Stand in front of it. Use a marking pen. Trace your face.
Sentences different lengths	Cut off a large piece of clear plastic wrap, and tape it to a mirror. Then stand in front of it. Use a marking pen to trace your face.

These two sets of instructions sound boring because the sentences are all the same length. Revise the instructions, using sentences of different lengths to make them more interesting.

1. Take two empty cans. Wash them out. Punch a hole in the bottom of each can. Connect the cans with string. Ask a friend to put one can up to an ear. Tell your friend to listen. Pull the string taut. Talk into the other can. Can your friend hear you?

_____

_____

_____

_____

_____

2. Find an empty cardboard tube. Hold it up to one eye. Keep both eyes open. Put one hand next to the tube. Hold the hand a few inches from your face. You will see a hole in your hand.

_____

_____

_____

_____

_____

Name _____

Finding the Best Information

What I Know	What I Want to Know	Possible Sources
Jesse Owens was a famous Olympic athlete.	When did he participate in the Olympics? What sport did he participate in?	*The Grolier Student Encyclopedia of the Olympic Games*, by Ron Thomas and Joe Herran
He worked with and helped young people.	What did he do, and how did he help?	*Jesse Owens*, by Tony Gentry

Read the following K-W-S chart for a research report on the Olympic Games. Then look at the sources listed in the box. Write the names of the sources that you think would provide the best information to answer the questions. When you write, underline the names in italics.

Weekly Reader	Olympics Web site
The Olympic Games, by Theodore Knight	*The Story of the Olympics*, by Dave Anderson
Microsoft Encarta Online Deluxe Encyclopedia	*Scholastic Kid's Almanac for the 21st Century*

K-W-S Chart

What I Know	What I Want to Know	Possible Sources
The Olympic Games began a long time ago.	When and how did the Olympic Games begin?	
Swimming and skiing are sports in the modern games.	What are some other sports that make up the games?	
The United States, China, and Russia participate in the games.	What are some other countries that send athletes to the games?	
The Summer Games were held in Sydney, Australia, in 2000.	When and where will the next Olympic Games be held?	

Grade 4: Unit 11 Research Report *(Use with pupil book pages 379-380.)*
Skill: Students will select the best sources to find information and then complete a K-W-S chart with the names of these sources.

UNIT 11 RESEARCH REPORT

Name _____

Writing from an Outline

Each section of an **outline** is about one main topic. When you write a **paragraph** from an outline, use the main topic to write a **topic sentence** for the paragraph. Write the subtopics as complete sentences that support the main idea.

The outline below is for a report on Earth's solar system. Write a paragraph from each outline section. Start by writing the topic sentence. Remember to indent each paragraph.

I. The moon, Earth's closest neighbor
   A. About one-quarter the size of Earth
   B. About two hundred thirty-nine thousand miles away
   C. Takes twenty-seven and one-third days to circle Earth
   D. Same side always faces Earth

_____

_____

_____

_____

_____

II. The sun, closest star to Earth
   A. Ninety-three million miles from Earth
   B. Sun's light reaches Earth in eight minutes
   C. Provides heat and light for life
   D. More than one hundred times the size of Earth

_____

_____

_____

_____

_____

_____

Grade 4: Unit 11   Research Report   *(Use with pupil book page 384.)*
Skill: Students will write paragraphs from outlines.

WORKBOOK PLUS
TCAP PRACTICE
147

Name _____

Good Openings and Closings

> A strong **opening** captures your reader's interest and tells what your report is about. A strong **closing** sums up the report and connects to the main idea.

1. Below are two possible openings and closings for a research report about the Loch Ness monster. Put a check beside the stronger opening and closing.

Openings

_____ I don't think there is a Loch Ness monster.

_____ Is some huge, mysterious creature lurking near the calm surface of a lovely Scottish lake?

Closings

_____ Maybe I will try to catch Nessie someday!

_____ Thus, the mystery of the Loch Ness monster still remains to be solved.

2. Write two good openings and two good closings for a report on icebergs using the outline. Ask a question and state a surprising fact. For the closing, try connecting to the main idea in the opening. Then put a check beside the opening and closing you think are stronger.

  I. Description of iceberg
    A. Mountain of ice floating in ocean
    B. Piece broken off glacier (huge field of ice)
    C. In summer, floats south from Arctic to Canada
  II. Size of iceberg
    A. Most of iceberg under water
    B. May be 400 feet above water
    C. Can be many miles long

Opening: _____

_____

Opening: _____

_____

Closing: _____

_____

Closing: _____

_____

© Houghton Mifflin Harcourt Publishing Company

Grade 4: Unit 11 Research Report *(Use with pupil book page 385.)*
Skill: Students will identify and will write strong openings and closings for a report on a given topic.

Name _____

Revising a Research Report

Have I   yes
- written a topic sentence using the main topic of the outline?   ❑
- arranged facts in an order that makes sense?   ❑
- added more facts from the outline?   ❑
- added details from the outline?   ❑
- crossed out sentences that give opinions?   ❑

Revise the following paragraph from a research report. Use the checklist above to help you. Check off each box when you have finished your revision. Use the outline section below to write a topic sentence. Use the spaces above the lines, on the sides, and below the paragraph for your changes.

II. Electric eels' use of electricity
  A. To hunt for food—fish and frogs
  B. Can stun an animal as big as a horse
  C. In place of eyesight, to find way around in muddy water
  D. To communicate with other electric eels, so some scientists think
  E. To protect self from enemies

An eel uses its electricity to hunt for food. The electricity can easily kill its food. It can even stun an animal. An eel also uses electricity to protect itself from enemies. I certainly wouldn't want to meet an electric eel in the water! After a while, electricity damages the eel's eyes, but the eel can use electricity to find its way around.

Grade 4: Unit 11   Research Report   (Use with pupil book page 386.)
Skill: Students will revise a paragraph for a research report, using a revision checklist.

WORKBOOK PLUS TCAP PRACTICE   149

Name _____

Elaborating: Details

Few details	The hummingbird beats its wings fast.
Elaborated with details	When gathering nectar, the hummingbird beats its wings more than 70 times a second, making a sort of humming sound.

Revise the supporting sentences in the paragraph below from a report on the ostrich, adding exact details from the picture and captions. The topic sentence is in dark print.

world's largest bird
almost 8 feet tall
can weigh up to 345 pounds

lives up to 70 years;
few birds live as long

lays eggs that
weigh 3 pounds

long legs
can run 40 miles
per hour

The ostrich is an unusual bird. It is very tall and weighs a lot. The ostrich cannot fly, but it can run fast. An ostrich hen lays big eggs. The ostrich lives a long time too.

The ostrich is an unusual bird. _____

_____

_____

_____

_____

_____

Grade 4: Unit 11 Research Report *(Use with pupil book page 388.)*
Skill: Students will revise a paragraph from a research report, elaborating with exact details.

Name _____

Supporting Sentences

An **opinion paragraph** tells what someone thinks or believes. It often has a focus statement, supporting sentences, and a concluding sentence. **Supporting sentences** give strong reasons for an opinion. They usually include facts and examples that make the reasons clear and convincing.

Complete the opinion paragraph about this picture. Write three supporting sentences that give reasons for the opinion presented in the focus statement below. Use details in the beach scene to elaborate each reason with facts and examples.

When you're ready for fun in the sun, a beach is the place to be!

_____

_____

_____

_____

_____

_____

_____

_____

_____

A beach is definitely the best place to spend a warm summer afternoon.

Name _____

Choosing Strong Reasons

Opinion: I don't like windy days.

Weak Reasons	Strong Reasons
general reason: feels cold **unimportant reason:** makes flags flutter	**exact reason:** icy chill makes me shiver **important reason:** makes it difficult to pedal my bike

In the T-Chart below, write three or four reasons why you like outdoor activities, and three or four reasons why you don't like them. Then cross out any reasons that are not important.

I like outdoor activities.	I do not like outdoor activities.

Grade 4: Unit 12 Opinion *(Use with pupil book page 423.)*
Skill: Students will choose strong reasons to support an opinion.

UNIT 12 OPINION

Name _____

Elaborating Your Reasons

Opinion: I like mystery stories.

Reason: Mystery stories challenge readers to think.

Weak Details	Strong Details
good plot	complex plot with twists and turns
interesting story	clues that help solve the mystery

Choose two reasons from the T-Chart about outdoor activities on the previous page and write them in the cluster below *Reasons*. Under *Details*, write details that make each reason more convincing.

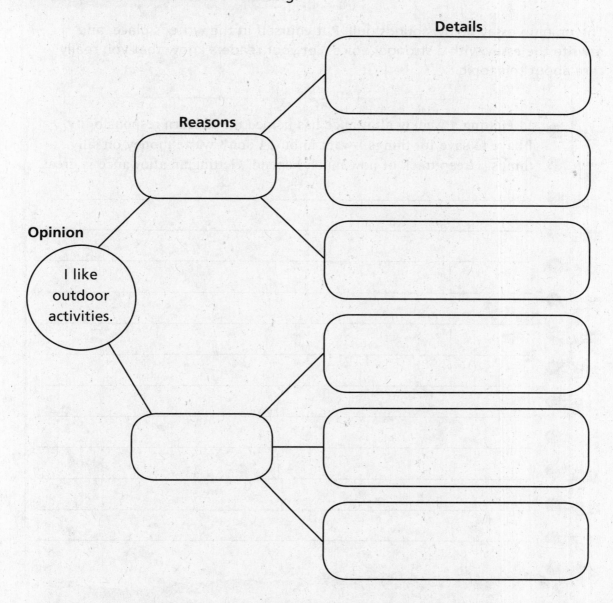

Details

Reasons

Opinion

I like outdoor activities.

Grade 4: Unit 12 Opinion *(Use with pupil book page 424.)*
   Skill: Students will identify reasons that support an opinion and choose
   details that elaborate those reasons.

WORKBOOK PLUS
TCAP PRACTICE **153**

Name _____

Writing with Voice

Weak Voice	Strong Voice
Airplane rides are nice. Taking off is the most exciting part. There are lots of different things to see. You get where you're going really fast.	Nothing beats the thrill of an airplane ride! The jet engines roar. The plane picks up speed on the runway, and I am pushed back against the seat by a tremendous force. Soaring high above the earth, I have a bird's-eye view of cities, farms, and rivers that wind across the landscape like ribbons. For traveling long distances, jet planes are the only way to go!

The opinion essay below sounds dull. Put yourself in the writer's place, and rewrite the essay with a stronger voice. Let your readers know that you really care about this topic.

Getting a weekly allowance has helped me to learn responsibility. I have to save for things I want to buy. I don't waste money on silly things. I keep track of how much I spend. Getting an allowance is great.

_____

_____

_____

_____

_____

_____

_____

_____

_____

_____

_____

_____

Grade 4: Unit 12   Opinion   *(Use with pupil book pages 425–426.)*
Skill: Students will rewrite an opinion essay, using strong voice.

Name _____

Openings and Closings

Weak Opening	Strong Opening
Here is why I like computers.	Have you ever considered the many ways that we use computers?

Weak Closing	Strong Closing
That's why I think computers are great.	Whether I'm searching for information, practicing my math, or playing games with a friend, computers are an important part of everyday life.

The short opinion essay below needs an opening. First, read the essay. Then write two strong openings. Read both your openings and decide which one you like best. Put a check mark in front of the stronger opening.

Every hockey game is packed with fast action. Players skate around the rink at a furious pace, passing the puck back and forth like a hot potato. A member of the home team fakes left, almost colliding with his opponent. Suddenly, the puck flies past the goalie, a light flashes behind the net, and the fans go wild. Only at a hockey rink will you experience action like this!

Strong Opening: _____

_____

Strong Opening: _____

_____

The opinion essay below needs a closing. First, read the paragraph. Then write two closings for it. Read both closings and decide which one you like better. Put a check mark in front of the stronger closing.

Whether I'm feeling a little bit blue or floating on top of the world, painting is my favorite way to share what I'm thinking and feeling. Creating pictures is my special way of showing others how I see the world. I love to play with different forms and shapes.

Strong Closing: _____

_____

Strong Closing: _____

_____

Grade 4: Unit 12   Opinion   *(Use with pupil book page 427.)*
   Skill: Students will write strong openings and closings for opinion essays.

WORKBOOK PLUS
TCAP PRACTICE   155

Revising an Opinion Essay

Have I	yes
• added an opening that introduces the topic and creates interest?	❏
• written a topic sentence that tells the main idea?	❏
• included strong reasons and details that support the opinion?	❏
• written in a way that sounds like me?	❏
• summed up the important points in the closing?	❏

Revise the following opinion essay to make it better. Use the checklist above to help you. Check off each box when you have finished your revision. You can use the spaces above the lines or the space around the paragraph to make your changes.

Baby-sitting

Baby-sitting is harder than it looks. When I baby-sit for five-year-old Carolyn, I am always on the go. When we play, she wants to do a dozen things at once. It was a beautiful sunny day. After ten minutes, I have to come up with something else to do. I watch her every move so that she doesn't fall and get hurt. She always needs something. She is hungry. Then she wants a drink. I read her a story. She begs for another. Carolyn never stops. I am always exhausted. Baby-sitting is a tough job.

Grade 4: Unit 12   Opinion   *(Use with pupil book page 428.)*
Skill: Students will revise an opinion essay, using a revision checklist.

Name _____

Elaborating: Word Choice

Without synonyms	The **big, pretty** snowflakes fell **fast**.
With synonyms	The **giant, lacy** snowflakes fell **swiftly**.

Revise the following opinion essay to make it more interesting. Underline words that seem too general or dull. Then rewrite the essay, replacing the underlined words with colorful synonyms that have a more exact meaning.

Volunteering to visit senior citizens is a good thing to do. A lot of elderly people feel bad because no one comes to see them. When someone takes time to talk to them, they are better. Listening to them tell about their experiences can be great. We can learn a lot from their stories. Most volunteers will tell you that they get back much more than they give when they help others.

_____

_____

_____

_____

_____

_____

_____

_____

_____

_____

_____

_____

_____

_____

_____

_____

_____

Grade 4: Unit 12 Opinion *(Use with pupil book page 430.)*
Skill: Students will revise an opinion essay, elaborating with synonyms.

**WORKBOOK PLUS
TCAP PRACTICE** 157

Name _____

Supporting Your Reasons

Reason: I should take up ice skating because skating is good for my body.

Weak Support	Strong Support
Opinion: Skating is good exercise. **Opinion**: Skating makes me feel good.	**Fact**: My doctor says the exercise I get while skating helps build strong muscles. **Example**: I can feel my heart beating faster when I skate.

Read the goal and reasons in the web below. Write two facts or examples that support each reason.

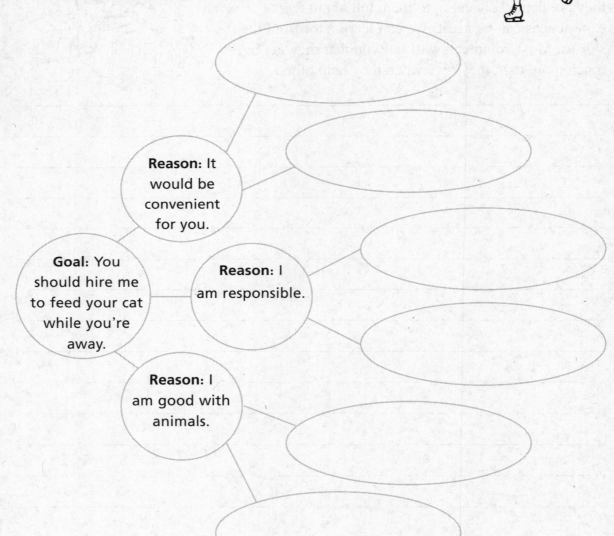

158 WORKBOOK PLUS
TCAP PRACTICE

Grade 4: Unit 13   Persuasion   *(Use with pupil book page 457.)*
Skill: Students will write facts and examples to support reasons.

Name _____

Evaluating Your Reasons

Goal: My principal should have a career day at school.

Reason for Principal	Reason for Students
Inviting adults to tell about their jobs will get the community involved with the school.	We would learn about a variety of jobs and careers.

Goal: My sister should let me borrow her bike.

Unconvincing Reason	Convincing Reason
I can't ride my bike.	My bike has a flat tire. The bike shop is closed.

Cross out the reasons below that do not show strong support or would not matter to the audience. Then fill in the web.

Reasons	Facts or Examples
My skills have improved.	running; ball handling
I am a team player.	willing to pass; don't need to be the star
I enjoy sporting events.	soccer; baseball
The team needs another member.	Mia quit the team; Zoe hurt her leg.
My parents go to all the games.	bring snacks; cheer loudly

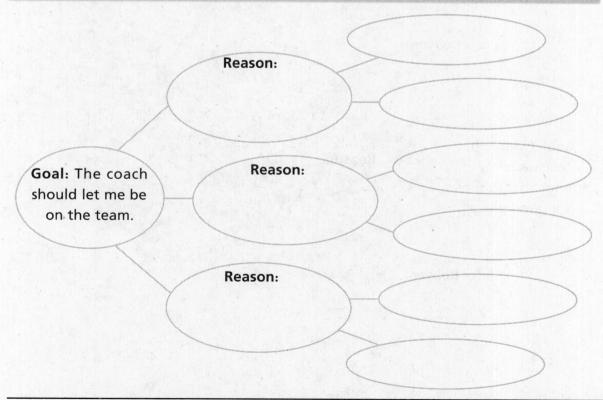

Reason:

Goal: The coach should let me be on the team.

Reason:

Reason:

Grade 4: Unit 13 Persuasion (*Use with pupil book page 458.*)
Skill: Students will choose strong support for a goal.

**WORKBOOK PLUS
TCAP PRACTICE** 159

Name _____

Organizing Your Essay

Goal: Mom should let my friend Zach stay for dinner.
2 Also, you made a big pot of spaghetti, so there's plenty of food.
The spaghetti smells delicious.
1 In the first place, we all like Zach and enjoy his funny stories.
3 Finally, you know how much Zach loves your spaghetti.

Three reasons for a persuasive essay are underlined below. Cross out the facts or examples that do not support the reasons. Number each reason 1, 2, or 3 to show the order in which you would write about them. Then organize the reasons and the facts and examples in the web below.

Goal: I want to persuade my friends that school is a good place to be.		
Reason ____ School is a caring place. Classmates made me get-well cards. Teacher gives me extra help. I sit in the front of the room.	**Reason** ____ We learn and do interesting things. winter and spring vacations fascinating field trips scientific experiments	**Reason** ____ Our friends are there too. play together during recess Martin is my friend. eat lunch together

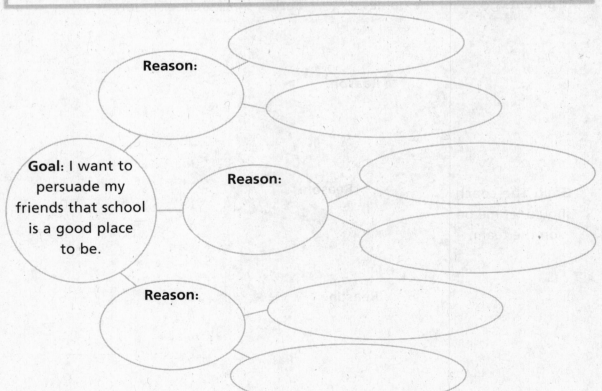

Grade 4: Unit 13 Persuasion (*Use with pupil book page 459.*)
 Skill: Students will organize reasons in order and choose facts and examples that support the reasons.

Name _____

Openings and Closings

Weak Opening	Strong Opening
The school band needs new uniforms. The present uniforms are old and shabby looking. We should raise money to buy new ones.	The school band sounds great. There's no reason why we can't look great too. We need new uniforms. Let's all pitch in and start that fundraising.

Weak Closing	Strong Closing
The band uniforms in this school need to be changed. It's embarrassing to wear them. We need to buy new ones.	Our band uniforms are old, faded, and in need of repair. Together we can do something about it. Let's organize and raise money to buy new uniforms!

Write two strong openings for persuasive essays about each goal below.

Goal: My mother should let me have a birthday party next month.

Opening: _____

_____

Opening: _____

_____

Goal: My friend should let me borrow her new T-shirt.

Opening: _____

_____

Opening: _____

_____

Goal: My grandmother should let me visit her this summer.

Opening: _____

_____

Opening: _____

_____

Grade 4: Unit 13 Persuasion *(Use with pupil book page 460.)*
Skill: Students will write strong openings for persuasive essays.

WORKBOOK PLUS
TCAP PRACTICE

161

Name _____

Writing with Voice

Weak: Negative Voice	Strong: Positive Voice
Our team is terrible! We haven't won a game this year. Without more practice sessions, I doubt if we ever will.	If we practice more and change our attitude, we'll get out of this slump. Our team is better than our record shows.

Weak: Not Confident Voice	Strong: Confident Voice
I think you should study more. Doing well in school is sort of important.	Success in school is a definite sign of how well you will do in the future. Clearly, studying prepares you for success.

The paragraph below isn't very persuasive. Rewrite the paragraph to give it a stronger voice. Show that your goal is important to you by adding words and phrases that persuade your reader. Then make sure you write a closing that sums up your goal and your reasons.

I think we should get a pet bird. First, a bird probably isn't hard to take care of. Second, a bird is quiet and would never bark at night. Finally, I think I'm old enough to take care of a pet. Most likely a bird would be the perfect pet.

_____

_____

_____

_____

_____

_____

_____

_____

_____

_____

Grade 4: Unit 13 Persuasion *(Use with pupil book page 461.)*
Skill: Students will rewrite a persuasive paragraph to give it a stronger voice.

Name _____

Revising a Persuasive Essay

Have I   **yes**
- made sure the goal is stated clearly?   ❏
- given strong reasons to support the goal?   ❏
- backed up the reasons with facts and examples?   ❏
- made sure the reasons stick to the topic?   ❏
- added a strong, positive voice?   ❏
- summed up the goals and reasons?   ❏

Revise the following persuasive essay to make it better. Use the checklist above to help you. Check off each box when you have finished your revision. You can use the spaces above the lines, on the sides, and below the paragraph for your changes.

Recycling Is Important

I think our school should begin a recycling program. First of all, recycling would reduce the amount of trash. Lots of trash is thrown away every day. Landfills are getting full. We have garbage pick-up twice a week. In addition, recycling at school would foster good habits. We would think twice before throwing things away. Finally, our school could earn some money. Some companies pay for things that can be recycled. A recycling program would help the environment and our school.

Grade 4: Unit 13   Persuasion   *(Use with pupil book page 462.)*
Skill: Students will revise a persuasive paragraph using a revision checklist.

**WORKBOOK PLUS
TCAP PRACTICE**   163

Name _____

Elaborating: Details

Few details	We can prevent injuries from skateboard accidents.
Elaborated with details	We can prevent ninety percent of the injuries from skateboard accidents by wearing safety helmets and knee and elbow pads.

Revise the persuasive writing below by adding vivid, descriptive details to make it more interesting.

My mom should let me do odd jobs for the neighbors. Most important, I could use the money to buy some things that I want. It would also save my mom money. Finally, it would keep me from being bored. Extra cash, savings for Mom, and something interesting for me to do are all good reasons for me to do odd jobs. Let the job hunt begin!

_____

_____

_____

_____

_____

_____

_____

_____

_____

_____

_____

_____

Grade 4: Unit 13 Persuasion *(Use with pupil book page 464.)*
Skill: Students will revise a persuasive paragraph, elaborating with descriptive details.

TCAP Practice

Tennessee Symbols   Week 1

Monday

1 **Read this sentence.**

I think Tennessee's flag is the _____ of all fifty state flags.

Which word or words best complete this sentence?

A handsomer

B handsomest

C most handsomest

D more handsomer

Tuesday

2 **Find the simple predicate, or action word, in the sentence.**

<u>Captain</u> LeRoy <u>Reeves</u> <u>designed</u> the state flag <u>of</u> Tennessee.

    F   **G**   **H**   **J**

Wednesday

3 **Read the two sentences.**

Tennessee's flag has three stars in a circle in the center. The stars are white.

What is the best way to combine these sentences?

A Tennessee's flag has three stars in a white circle in the center.

B Tennessee's flag has three stars in a circle in the center, they are white.

C Tennessee's flag has three white stars in a circle in the center.

D Tennessee's flag has three stars in a circle the center, and the stars are white.

Tennessee Symbols

Thursday

4 **Look at the underlined part of the sentence.**

Jake <u>asked "what</u> do the stars on Tennessee's flag stand for?"

Which answer shows the correct capitalization and punctuation for the underlined part?

F asked, "What

G asked "What

H asked, "what

J Correct as it is

Friday

5 **Find the sentence that is complete and written correctly.**

A The meaning of the stars on Tennessee's flag.

B They stand for the state's three main areas.

C East Tennessee, Middle Tennessee, and West Tennessee.

D Have different landforms, climates, and ways of life.

Journal Writing Ideas

- What symbols would you put on a flag for your school or community? Why?

- What are some of the different ways in which people use flags?

Tennessee Symbols   Week 2

Monday

1 **Read this sentence.**

Yesterday a mockingbird _____ outside my window.

Which word or words best complete this sentence?

A sing

B sung

C has sang

D sang

Tuesday

2 **Find the simple predicate, or action word, in the sentence.**

<u>Tennessee</u> <u>chose</u> the mockingbird <u>as</u> its <u>official</u> state bird.

    F   **G**   **H**   **J**

Wednesday

3 **Which sentence is written correctly?**

A Have you ever heard a mockingbird.

B It is one of the most musical birds in North America.

C In addition to its own call. It copies those of other birds.

D What a talented singer the mockingbird is?

Tennessee Symbols

Read this paragraph. Then answer Numbers 4 and 5.

> [1]The mockingbird is about the size of a robin, with a light gray breast, dark gray wings, and a long tail. [2]It has bits of white on its wings. [3]It has bits of white on its tail. [4]The mockingbird is lively, curious, and charming. [5]No wonder five states select it as their state bird!

Thursday

4 **What is the best way to combine Sentence 2 and Sentence 3?**

F It has bits of white on its wings and a white tail.

G It has bits of white on its wings, and it has bits of white on its tail.

H It has bits of white on its wings, it has them on its tail too.

J It has bits of white on its wings and tail.

Friday

5 **What is the best way to write Sentence 5?**

A No wonder five states selecting it as their state bird!

B No wonder five states selected it as their state bird!

C No wonder five states been selecting it as their state bird!

D Correct as it is

Journal Writing Ideas

- What bird would you choose as a symbol for yourself? Why?
- Describe a bird that you often see near your home.

Tennessee Symbols

Monday

1 **Which sentence is written correctly?**

A Did you know that Tennessee has an official state painting.

B It shows a forest scene with several plants and animals that are symbols of Tennessee.

C The artist is michael Sloan, who studied at the Memphis College of Art.

D Sloan was a featured artist at the 1982 World's Fair in Knoxville Tennessee.

Tuesday

2 **Look at the underlined part of the sentence.**

Tennessee adopted its first official state <u>painting, *Tennessee Treasures*, in</u> 1997.

Which answer shows the correct capitalization and punctuation for the underlined part?

F painting *tennessee treasures* in

G painting *Tennessee treasures*, in

H painting, *Tennessee Treasures* in

J Correct as it is

Wednesday

3 **Read this sentence.**

Sloan's paintings of Tennessee are the _____ ones I've ever seen!

Which word or words best complete this sentence?

A bestest   **C** best

B most best   **D** most good

Tennessee Symbols

Read the passage and look at the numbered, underlined parts. For Numbers 4 and 5, choose the answer that shows the correct capitalization and punctuation for each underlined part.

> Tennessee's first official painting shows ten of the state's <u>symbols, some</u>
> (4)
> of the animal symbols in this forest scene are a raccoon, a mockingbird, and
>
> a <u>ladybug. The</u> scene also includes a Tennessee River pearl, some blue irises, and
> (5)
> a tulip poplar tree.

Thursday

4 **F** symbols. Some

   G symbols some

   H symbols, Some

   J Correct as it is

Friday

5 **A** ladybug, the

   B ladybug? The

   C ladybug the

   D Correct as it is

Journal Writing Ideas

- If you were to paint something that is important to you about Tennessee, what would it be? Explain why it's important to you.

- Tell about an art project that you enjoyed doing.

Tennessee Symbols

Monday

1 **Read this sentence.**

What fish and gem _____ as Tennessee state symbols?

Which word or words best complete this sentence?

A   chosen

B   were chose

C   choosed

D   were chosen

Tuesday

2 **Find the simple predicate, or action word, in the sentence.**

Tennessee state <u>officials</u> <u>picked</u> the largemouth bass and the
                               F   **G**

Tennessee <u>River</u> pearl as <u>two</u> of its symbols.
           H   **J**

Wednesday

3 **Find the sentence that is complete and written correctly.**

A   The big, tasty largemouth bass.

B   Found in most of Tennessee's lakes and streams.

C   Tennessee River pearls form in mussel shells.

D   Their soft, pretty colors and unusual shapes.

Tennessee Symbols

For Numbers 4 and 5, choose the answer that shows the correct capitalization and punctuation to complete this information from a website.

Visiting Tennessee?

Learn about Tennessee River pearls at

Freshwater Pearl Farm and Museum

255 Marina Road

_____

(4)

Fish for largemouth bass at

Norris Dam State Park

125 Village Green Circle

_____

(5)

Thursday

4
F Camden TN, 38320	**H** Camden, TN 38320
G Camden, TN, 38320	**J** Camden TN 38320

Friday

5
A Lake city, TN 37769	**C** Lake city, Tn 37769
B Lake City, tn 37769	**D** Lake City, TN 37769

Journal Writing Ideas

- Describe a gemstone that you think is beautiful.
- Write everything you know about a kind of fish or another kind creature that lives in water.

Tennessee Places   Week 5

Monday

1 **Read this sentence.**

Nashville _____ the capital of Tennessee in 1843.

Which word or words best complete this sentence?

A become

B had became

C becoming

D became

Tuesday

2 **Find the sentence that is complete and written correctly.**

F Nashville famous as the home of the Grand Ole Opry.

G The city lies along the Cumberland River.

H Has the second-largest population of Tennessee cities.

J Health care the biggest industry in Nashville.

Wednesday

3 **Find the simple predicate, or action word, of the sentence.**

Many <u>companies</u> in Nashville <u>produce</u> <u>music</u> and books.

      A   **B**   **C**   **D**

Tennessee Places

Read this paragraph. Then answer Numbers 4 and 5.

> [1]Nashville is an exciting place to live. [2]Like Athens in ancient Greece, it is a center for culture. [3]Art and music are important there. [4]Learning is also important there. [5]Nashville be called the Athens of the South.

Thursday

4 **What is the best way to combine Sentences 3 and 4?**

  F Art and music are important, and learning is also important.

  G Art and music are important there, and learning is also important there.

  H Art, music, and learning are important there.

  J Art and music and learning are important there.

Friday

5 **What is the best way to write Sentence 5?**

  A Nashville is called the Athens of the South.

  B Nashville been called the Athens of the South.

  C Nashville are called the Athens of the South.

  D Correct as it is

Journal Writing Ideas

- Write about an interesting kind of business or entertainment in your town or city.

- Describe a natural feature such as a mountain or river in or near your town or city.

Tennessee Places Week 6

Monday

1 **Which sentence is written correctly?**

   A   James winchester founded the city of Memphis.

   B   Winchester had fought in the american revoluton.

   C   He named Memphis after a city in ancient Egypt.

   D   Like the ancient city, the new one lay on a great river?

Tuesday

2 **Look at the underlined part of the sentence.**

   Josh <u>said, "The</u> city of Memphis is on the Mississippi River."

   Which answer shows the correct capitalization and punctuation for the underlined part?

   F   said", The

   G   said, "the

   H   said "The

   J   Correct as it is

Wednesday

3 **Read this sentence.**

   Memphis is the _____ of all the cities in Tennessee.

   Which word or words best complete this sentence?

   A   most large

   B   largest

   C   most largest

   D   larger

© Houghton Mifflin Harcourt Publishing Company

Name _____

Tennessee Places

Thursday

 Find the simple subject, or naming word, of the sentence below.

<u>Our</u> <u>teacher</u> <u>showed</u> us a <u>map</u> of Memphis.

   F   **G**   **H**   **J**

Friday

 Read the two sentences.

Memphis has a port on the Mississippi River. The port is busy.

What is the <u>best</u> way to combine these sentences?

A   Memphis has a port on the busy Mississippi River.

B   Memphis has a port on the Mississippi River, and the port is busy.

C   Memphis has a busy port on the Mississippi River.

D   Memphis has a port on the Mississippi River it is busy.

Journal Writing Ideas

• Would you rather live in a big city or in the country? Why?

• Why do you think being located on a river can help the population of a city to grow?

Tennessee Places   Week 7

Monday

1 **Read the two sentences.**

Knoxville was named for Henry Knox. Knox was a general.

What is the <u>best</u> way to combine these sentences?

A   Knoxville was named for Henry Knox, and Knox was a general.

B   Knoxville was named for General Henry Knox.

C   Knoxville was named for a general who was named Henry Knox

D   Knoxville was named General Henry Knox.

Tuesday

2 **Read this sentence.**

The railroad helped to _____ Knoxville an important city.

Which word <u>best</u> completes this sentence?

F   makes   **H**   making

G   made   **J**   make

Wednesday

3 **Look at the underlined part of the sentence.**

<u>Isnt Knoxville</u> where the East Tennessee History Center is located?

Which answer shows the correct capitalization and punctuation for the underlined part?

A   Isn't Knoxville

B   isn't knoxville

C   Is'nt Knoxville

D   Correct as it is

© Houghton Mifflin Harcourt Publishing Company

Tennessee Places

For Numbers 4 and 5, choose the answer that shows the correct capitalization and punctuation to complete this information from a website.

East Tennessee History Center

10:00 a.m. to 4:00 p.m.

_____

(4)

601 South Gay Street

_____

(5)

Thursday

4 **F** monday through saturday

G Monday through saturday

H monday through Saturday

J Monday through Saturday

Friday

5 **A** Knoxville Tennessee **C** Knoxville, Tennessee

B Knoxville, tennessee **D** knoxville tennessee

Journal Writing Ideas

• What are some reasons why people might name their town or city after a certain person?

• How do you think your town or city may have been different a hundred years ago?

Tennessee Cities

Monday

1 **Which sentence is written correctly?**

A   The town of Tullahoma has an interesting name

B   The town gets its name from a Choctaw word.

C   Tullahoma is about 40 miles west of chattanooga.

D   Its the only United States city with that name.

Tuesday

2 **Find the sentence that is complete and written correctly.**

F   Fishing in many large lakes.

G   Catching many kinds of fish?

H   We went out in a boat.

J   A sunny day but not too warm.

Wednesday

3 **Read this sentence.**

We _____ on a fishing trip.

Which word or words best complete this sentence?

A   goed

B   has gone

C   went

D   going

Tennessee Cities

Week 8 (continued)

Read the passage and look at the numbered, underlined parts. For Numbers 4 and 5, choose the answer that shows the correct capitalization and punctuation for each underlined part.

The area around Tullahoma is known for its schools and its beauty, nearby
                                                                   (4)
Ledford's Mill is a popular place to visit, Ledford's Mill was built around 1884
                                         (5)
and is now an inn.

Thursday

4   **F**   beauty. Nearby

     G   beauty nearby

     H   Beauty. Nearby

     J   Correct as it is

Friday

5   **A**   visit, ledford's

     B   visit. Ledford's

     C   Visit, Ledford's

     D   Correct as it is

Journal Writing Ideas

- Describe the most unusual Tennessee town or city that you have ever visited.

- If you were to go on vacation in Tennessee, where would you go? Why?

Tennessee People

Monday

1 **Find the simple predicate, or action word, of the sentence below.**

Anne Dallas Dudley believed in equal rights for women.

　　A　　　　 B　　 C　 D

Tuesday

2 **Look at the underlined part of the sentence.**

Anne Dallas Dudley lived in nashville, Tennessee.

Which answer shows the correct capitalization and punctuation for the underlined part?

F Nashville Tennessee.

G nashville Tennessee.

H Nashville, Tennessee.

J Correct as it is

Wednesday

3 **Find the sentence that is complete and written correctly.**

A Anne Dallas Dudley in the National Women's Hall of Fame.

B Grew up during the late 1800s.

C A champion of women's voting rights.

D Only men could vote in Tennessee at that time.

Tennessee People

Read the passage and look at the numbered, underlined parts. For Numbers
4 and 5, choose the answer that shows the correct capitalization and punctuation
for each underlined part.

> Anne Dallas Dudley campaigned for a new law. This law would give women
>
> the right to <u>vote Dudley</u> gave persuasive speeches all over the <u>South, and she</u>
>   **(4)**   **(5)**
>
> helped the law to pass.

Thursday

4   **F**   vote. Dudley

      G   vote, Dudley

      H   vote? Dudley

      J   Correct as it is

Friday

5   **A**   South. and she

      B   South and she

      C   South. And she

      D   Correct as it is

Journal Writing Ideas

- Write about a new rule that you would like in your home, school, or
  community. Explain why your rule is a fair one.

- Write about a time when you or someone you know helped to improve an
  unfair situation.

Tennessee Heroes

Monday

1 **Read the two sentences.**

Andrew Jackson was a president. He was from Tennessee.

What is the best way to combine these sentences?

A   From Tennessee was President Andrew Jackson.

B   Andrew Jackson was a president, and he was from Tennessee.

C   President Andrew Jackson was from Tennessee.

D   Andrew Jackson from Tennessee was a president.

Tuesday

2 **Find the sentence that is complete and written correctly.**

F   Learned that he was the hero of the Battle of New Orleans.

G   Elected to the House of Representatives.

H   He also served as a senator.

J   Became our seventh president.

Wednesday

3 **Read this sentence.**

Jackson _____ two terms as president.

Which word or words best complete this sentence?

A   serve

B   have served

C   served

D   serving

Tennessee Heroes

Week 10 (continued)

Read this paragraph. Then answer Numbers 4 and 5.

> ¹Jackson's first home was a log cabin. ²He later builts a large mansion called the Hermitage. ³Jackson lived there much of his life. ⁴Jackson's wife Rachel is buried at the Hermitage. ⁵Jackson is buried at the Hermitage.

Thursday

4 What is the <u>best</u> way to write Sentence 2?

   F He later builded a large mansion called the Hermitage.

   G He later built a large mansion calls the Hermitage.

   H He later built a large mansion called the Hermitage.

   J Best as it is

Friday

5 What is the <u>best</u> way to combine Sentences 3 and 4?

   A Jackson and his wife Rachel are buried at the Hermitage.

   B Jackson is buried at the Hermitage and his wife Rachel.

   C At the Hermitage, Jackson is buried and his wife Rachel.

   D Jackson is buried and his wife Rachel at the Hermitage.

Journal Writing Ideas

- Andrew Jackson was called Old Hickory because he was as hard and as tough as a hickory tree. What nickname would you choose for yourself? Why?

- Describe someone who is a hero to you, and tell what that person did to become a hero.

Tennessee People   Week 11

Monday

1 **Read this sentence.**

The Cherokee people _____ Nancy Ward "Beloved Woman."

Which word or words best complete this sentence?

A   calls

B   called

C   have call

D   is calling

Tuesday

2 **Find the sentence that is complete and written correctly.**

F   Nancy Ward, an important Cherokee leader.

G   Born in Chota, Tennessee, in 1738.

H   Her Cherokee name was Nanye-hi.

J   A member of the Council of Chiefs.

Wednesday

3 **Which sentence is written correctly?**

A   Nancy Ward fought beside her husband in battle

B   She led a successful charge against the Creeks.

C   Later, she promoted peace with european settlers.

D   Ward was a strong courageous, and wise leader.

Tennessee People

Read this paragraph. Then answer Numbers 4 and 5.

> [1]White settlers had brung new conflict to Cherokee lands. [2]Ward made peace. [3]She said, "Let your women's sons be ours. Let our sons be yours." [4]Sadly, the treaty was soon broken. [5]Yet, her words are remembered. [6]Her words are powerful.

Thursday

4 What is the <u>best</u> way to write Sentence 1?

F White settlers brang new conflict to Cherokee lands.

G White settlers brung new conflict to Cherokee lands.

H White settlers had brought new conflict to Cherokee lands.

J Correct as it is

Friday

5 What is the <u>best</u> way to combine Sentences 5 and 6?

A Yet, her words are remembered, and her words are powerful.

B Yet, her words are remembered, and are powerful.

C Yet, her words are remembered, her words are powerful.

D Yet, her powerful words are remembered.

Journal Writing Ideas

- Why do you think Nancy Ward preferred peace to war?

- Tell about a time when you solved a conflict in a peaceful way.

Tennessee Heroes

Monday

1 **Read the two sentences.**

Casey Jones was a railroad engineer.

He crashed his train into a freight train.

What is the <u>best</u> way to combine these sentences?

A Casey Jones crashed his train into a freight train, a railroad engineer.

B Casey Jones was a railroad engineer, and he crashed his train into a freight train.

C Casey Jones, a railroad engineer, crashed his train into a freight train.

D Into a freight train, Casey Jones, a railroad engineer, crashed his train.

Tuesday

2 **Find the simple subject, or naming word, of the sentence below.**

The <u>train</u> <u>crashed</u> early in the <u>morning</u> of <u>April 30, 1900</u>.

F   **G**   **H**   **J**

Wednesday

3 **Read this sentence.**

Soon people _____ singing songs about Casey.

Which word or words <u>best</u> complete this sentence?

A start

B started

C has started

D starting

© Houghton Mifflin Harcourt Publishing Company

Tennessee Heroes

For Numbers 4 and 5, choose the answer that shows the correct capitalization and punctuation to complete the sign.

Make up a new verse to "The Ballad of Casey Jones."

Please send your verse to Radio Station WXYZ _____ 37202

(4)

Entries must be received by _____.

(5)

Ten winners will receive a train engineer's hat.

Thursday

4 **F** Nashville, TN

G Nashville TN.

H Nashville; TN

J Nashville, TN,

Friday

5 **A** April, 30, 2008

B April, 30 2008

C April 30 2008,

D April 30, 2008

Journal Writing Ideas

• Who would you write a song about? Why?

• Try writing a song about yourself. Choose any tune, and create your own lyrics to accompany the music.

Tennessee Music

Monday

1 **Read this sentence.**

Today country singer Kitty Wells is _____ than Elvis.

Which word or words best complete this sentence?

A least well known

B less well known

C leastest well known

D littler well known

Tuesday

2 **Look at the underlined part of the sentence.**

Emily asked, "Why is Kitty Wells important to country <u>music"</u>.

Which answer shows the correct punctuation for the underlined part?

F music"?

G music."

H music?"

J Correct as it is

Wednesday

3 **Find the sentence that is complete and written correctly.**

A Country music pioneer Kitty Wells.

B Learned to sing and play the guitar when young.

C Recorded the first number-one country hit by a woman.

D She helped open country music to women.

Tennessee Music

Week 13 (continued)

Read the passage and look at the numbered, underlined parts. For Numbers
4 and 5, choose the answer that shows the correct capitalization and punctuation
for each underlined part.

> Kitty Wells is known as the Queen of Country <u>Music, She</u> was born on
> (4)
> August 30, 1919, in Nashville. During her career, Wells recorded more than
>
> twenty number-one <u>hits singers</u> such as Loretta Lynn followed in her footsteps.
> (5)

Thursday

4 **F** Music. She

    G Music she

    H Music, she

    J Correct as it is

Friday

5 **A** hits, Singers

    B hits. Singers

    C hits, singers

    D Correct as it is

Journal Writing Ideas

- Would you like to be a famous singer? Why or why not?
- What is your favorite kind of music? Why do you enjoy listening to it?

Tennessee Music

Monday

1 **Find the simple predicate, or action word, of the sentence below.**

Do <u>you</u> <u>listen</u> <u>to</u> country <u>music</u>?

    A **B** **C**   **D**

Tuesday

2 **Find the sentence that is complete and written correctly.**

F   Going to the Grand Ole Opry.

G   Need to get tickets?

H   I hope to see someone famous.

J   Hear many great singers.

Wednesday

3 **Read this sentence.**

Grand Ole Opry is a show that is _____ than you or your parents.

Which word or words best complete this sentence?

A   old

B   older

C   oldest

D   more older

© Houghton Mifflin Harcourt Publishing Company

Tennessee Music

Read this paragraph. Then answer Numbers 4 and 5.

> [1]Grand Ole Opry began as a radio program. [2]Grand Ole Opry began in 1925. [3]Nearly every famous country musician has performed on it. [4]People from around the world visit the Grand Ole Opry.

Thursday

4 **What is the _best_ way to combine Sentences 1 and 2?**

   F   Grand Ole Opry began as a radio program and began in 1925.

   G   Grand Ole Opry began as a radio program and in 1925.

   H   Grand Ole Opry began as a radio program in 1925.

   J   In radio, Grand Ole Opry began as a 1925 program.

Friday

5 **What is the _best_ way to write Sentence 4?**

   A   People from around the world visits the Grand Ole Opry.

   B   People from around the world visiting the Grand Ole Opry.

   C   People from around the world has visited the Grand Ole Opry.

   D   Best as it is

Journal Writing Ideas

- What musical instruments do you like to listen to?

- Would you like to go to the Grand Ole Opry? What do you think it would be like?

Tennessee Music

Monday

1 **Find the simple predicate, or action word, in the sentence.**

Thousands of Elvis Presley fans visit Graceland every year.
    A   **B**   **C**   **D**

Tuesday

2 **Find the sentence that is complete and written correctly.**

F Won second place in a talent show when he was ten years old.

G The prize was five dollars.

H A truck driver when he recorded his first song.

J Elvis known around the world as "The King of Rock and Roll."

Wednesday

3 **Which sentence is written correctly?**

A Elvis was born in tupelo, Mississippi.

B Graceland was his home in Memphis Tennessee.

C Elvis changed the sound of music in the United states

D His music is popular with many different age groups.

© Houghton Mifflin Harcourt Publishing Company

Tennessee Music

For Numbers 4 and 5, choose the answer that shows the correct capitalization and punctuation to complete the sign.

Welcome to Graceland, home of Elvis Presley.
_____ Memphis, Tennessee.
(4)

Elvis was born _____.
(5)

Join us for the Elvis Presley birthday celebration each January.

Thursday

4 F 3734 elvis Presley Boulevard

G 3734 Elvis presley Boulevard

H 3734 Elvis Presley boulevard

J 3734 Elvis Presley Boulevard

Friday

5 A January 8, 1935   C January, 8 1935

B January, 8, 1935   D January 8 1935

Journal Writing Ideas

- Elvis named his home Graceland. What would be a good name for your home? Why?

- Write about what it would be like to be a famous person?

Tennessee Music

Monday

1 **Read the two sentences.**

Dolly Parton is a singer and songwriter. She is talented.

What is the best way to combine these sentences?

A   Dolly Parton is a talented singer and a talented songwriter.

B   Dolly Parton is a talented songwriter.

C   Dolly Parton is a singer and songwriter, and she is talented.

D   Dolly Parton is a talented singer and songwriter.

Tuesday

2 **Find the sentence that is complete and written correctly.**

F   The amazing career of Dolly Parton!

G   Grew up in a poor family in Sevier County, Tennessee.

H   She was the fourth of twelve children.

J   Dreamed of becoming a famous singer.

Wednesday

3 **Look at the underlined part of the sentence.**

Tyler <u>said, By</u> age ten, Dolly Parton was singing on TV."

Which answer shows the correct capitalization and punctuation for the underlined part?

A   said "By

B   said, "by

C   said, "By

D   Correct as it is

Name _____

Tennessee Music

Thursday

 Find the simple predicate, or action word, of the sentence below.

<u>Dolly Parton</u> <u>also</u> <u>created</u> the theme <u>park</u> Dollywood.

     F   **G**   **H**   **J**

Friday

5 **Read this sentence.**

Tyler thinks Dolly Parton is _____ than Elvis Presley.

Which word or words best complete this sentence?

A   wonderfuler

B   more wonderful

C   most wonderful

D   more wonderfuler

Journal Writing Ideas

- Write about one of your talents.

- What kind of success do you dream about? What would it be like to achieve your dreams?

Tennessee Civil War

Monday

1 **Read the two sentences.**

Abraham Lincoln was elected president. The election was in the year 1860.

What is the best way to combine these sentences?

A   Abraham Lincoln was elected president and the election was in the year 1860.

B   Abraham Lincoln was elected in the year 1860 president.

C   Abraham Lincoln was elected president in the year 1860.

D   Abraham Lincoln in the year 1860 was elected president.

Tuesday

2 **Which sentence is written correctly?**

F   Many people in the South were not Happy when he was elected.

G   South carolina, Mississippi, Georgia, and other states decided to leave the Union.

H   Tennessee voted on february, 9 1861.

J   The state would remain in the Union.

Wednesday

3 **Read this sentence.**

Shots _____ at Fort Sumter, South Carolina.

Which word or words best complete this sentence?

A   being fired

B   fired

C   were fired

D   firing

© Houghton Mifflin Harcourt Publishing Company

Name _____

Tennessee Civil War

Read the passage and look at the numbered, underlined parts. For Numbers 4 and 5, choose the answer that shows the correct capitalization and punctuation for each underlined part.

> Tennessee voted again on June 8, <u>1861, this</u> time, the state joined the
> (4)
> Confederacy. Tennessee's hills and valleys soon became <u>Civil war</u> battlefields.
> (5)

Thursday

4 **F** 1861 this

    G 1861. This

    H 1861. this

    J Correct as it is

Friday

5 **A** Civil War

    B civil war

    C civil War

    D Correct as it is

Journal Writing Ideas

- Write about a disagreement you had with someone. What was the problem? How did you solve it?

- Do you ever see signs of the Civil War around you? When? Where?

Tennessee Civil War   Week 18

Monday

1 **Find the simple predicate, or action word, of the sentence below.**

Civil War <u>soldiers</u> <u>fought</u> <u>at</u> <u>Fort Henry</u> in Tennessee.

        A   **B**   **C**   **D**

Tuesday

2 **Find the sentence that is complete and written correctly.**

F   Fort Henry, not far from Clarkesville, Tennessee.

G   Site of a major victory for the North.

H   Flooding at the fort during the battle.

J   The fort now lies beneath Kentucky Lake.

Wednesday

3 **Read this sentence.**

General Tilghman _____ the Confederate troops at Fort Henry.

Which word or words best complete this sentence?

A   has led

B   led

C   leading

D   have led

Name _____

Tennessee Civil War

Read this paragraph. Then answer Numbers 4 and 5.

> [1]General Grant planned to attack Fort Henry. [2]He moved 15,000 Union troops near the fort. [3]General Tilghman quickly saw that he could not win and decided to withdraw most of his men. [4]He sent themselves east to Fort Donelson.

Thursday

4 What is the <u>best</u> way to combine Sentences 1 and 2?

F General Grant planned to attack Fort Henry, and General Grant moved 15,000 Union troops near the fort.

G General Grant planned to attack 15,000 Union troops near Fort Henry.

H General Grant planned to attack Fort Henry, so he moved 15,000 Union troops near the fort.

J General Grant planned to attack Fort Henry because he moved 15,000 Union troops near the fort.

Friday

5 What is the <u>best</u> way to write Sentence 4?

A He sent thems east to Fort Donelson.

B He sent them east to Fort Donelson.

C He sent they east to Fort Donelson.

D Correct as it is

Journal Writing Ideas

- If you were a general, what would you say to your troops before a battle?
- Tell about a time when you had to face a difficult challenge.

Tennessee Civil War

Monday

1 **Read this sentence.**

Nothing _____ between Union troops and the capital of Tennessee in early 1862.

Which word or words best complete this sentence?

A stand

B were standing

C standing

D stood

Tuesday

2 **Find the sentence that is complete and written correctly.**

F General Grant closer to Nashville.

G Could Nashville hold off the Northern armies?

H The Northern soldiers into the city on February 25.

J Had control of the center of the state.

Wednesday

3 **Find the simple predicate, or action word, of the sentence below.**

The Confederacy lost Nashville to Union troops.
      A   **B**   **C**   **D**

Tennessee Civil War

Thursday

4 **Read the two sentences.**

People left Nashville by train and by wagon. They left Nashville on foot.

What is the best way to combine these sentences?

F People left Nashville by train, by wagon, and on foot.

G People left Nashville on foot, and they left Nashville by train and by wagon.

H People left Nashville by train and by wagon and on foot.

J On foot people left Nashville and by train and by wagon.

Friday

5 **Look at the underlined part of the sentence.**

The <u>governor escaped? So</u> the mayor surrendered to the Union troops.

Which answer shows the correct capitalization and punctuation for the underlined part?

A governor escaped, so

B governor escaped, So

C governor escaped. so

D Correct as it is

Journal Writing Ideas

- Create a "recipe" for peace in your journal. List your ingredients, and write instructions on how to make peace.

- Describe what you think it would have been like to be a soldier in the Civil War.

Name _____

Tennessee Civil War

Week 20

Monday

1 **Look at the underlined part of the sentence.**

In the spring of <u>1862 Memphis</u> was held by Southern troops.

Which answer shows the correct capitalization and punctuation for the underlined part?

A   1862. Memphis

B   1862, memphis

C   1862, Memphis

D   Correct as it is

Tuesday

2 **Read this sentence.**

Northern soldiers _____ the flag over the courthouse in June.

Which word or words best complete this sentence?

F   raises

G   raised

H   will rise

J   was raising

Wednesday

3 **Find the sentence that is complete and written correctly.**

A   Memphis being on the Mississippi River.

B   The mayor of Memphis surrendered to the Union army.

C   Mississippi River in control of the North.

D   The Union troops in Tennessee.

Tennessee Civil War

Week 20 (continued)

For Numbers 4 and 5, choose the answer that shows the correct capitalization and punctuation to complete the sign.

> The naval battle of _____ was fought on _____. The battle lasted a
> little over an hour. Union guns sank every Confederate ship but one and took
> control of the city.
>
> (4) (5)

Thursday

4 F   memphis, tennessee

     G   Memphis tennessee

     H   memphis, Tennessee

     J   Memphis, Tennessee

Friday

5 A   June, 6, 1862

     B   June 6, 1862

     C   June 6; 1862

     D   June 6 1862

Journal Writing Ideas

- How is a big river like a highway?
- What do you think you would see and hear as you travel down a river on a riverboat?

Tennessee Geography   Week 21

Monday

1 **Read this sentence.**

Geography teaches _____ about land and the life on it.

Which word best completes this sentence?

A we

B ourselves

C us

D he

Tuesday

2 **Find the sentence that is complete and written correctly.**

F Soil, river, and mountains all part of geography.

G The Appalachian Mountains through our state.

H Some of the peaks 6,000 feet high.

J They were not easy for pioneers to climb.

Wednesday

3 **Which sentence is written correctly?**

A No one could easily cross the Unaka mountains long ago

B Today, Roads crisscross the mountains.

C The mountains are beautiful in the fall?

D Red Fork Falls is a 60-foot waterfall.

Tennessee Geography

Read this paragraph. Then answer Numbers 4 and 5.

> ¹Our teacher show us pictures of her camping trip. ²She went backpacking in the Unaka Mountains. ³She hiked on Limestone Cove Trail.

Thursday

4 What is the <u>best</u> way to write Sentence 1?

   F   Our teacher showed us pictures of her camping trip.

   G   Our teacher shown us pictures of her camping trip.

   H   Our teacher shows us pictures of she camping trip.

   J   Best as it is

Friday

5 What is the <u>best</u> way to combine Sentences 2 and 3?

   A   She hiked on Limestone Cove Trail but went backpacking in the Unaka Mountains.

   B   Hiking on Limestone Cove Trail and backpacking in the Unaka Mountains.

   C   She went backpacking in the Unaka Mountains and hiked on Limestone Cove Trail.

   D   She hiked on the Limestone Cove Trail and backpacking in the Unaka Mountains.

Journal Writing Ideas

- What would you take with you if you went hiking in the Unaka Mountains?

- Have you ever gone exploring? Write about that time.

Tennessee Geography   Week 22

Monday

1 **Look at the underlined part of the sentence.**

"How beautiful the Tennessee River <u>is"! said Ashley.</u>

Which answer shows the correct punctuation for the underlined part?

A   is!" said Ashley.

B   is" said Ashley!

C   is"! said Ashley

D   Correct as it

Tuesday

2 **Read the two sentences.**

Ashley went rowing with her brother on the Tennessee River. Her brother is Ethan.

What is the <u>best</u> way to combine these sentences?

F   Ashley and her brother went rowing on the Tennessee River.

G   Ashley went rowing with Ethan on the Tennessee River.

H   Ashley went rowing with her brother, Ethan, on the Tennessee River.

J   Ashley went rowing with her brother and Ethan on the Tennessee River.

Wednesday

3 **Find the sentence that is complete and written correctly.**

A   Important resources from the Tennessee River.

B   To water crops and to produce electricity.

C   People also use the river for pleasure.

D   Fishing, swimming, and boating.

Tennessee Geography

Thursday

4 **Which sentence is written correctly?**

    F   Can you name a lake in Tennessee?

    G   Reelfoot lake is in northwestern Tennessee.

    H   The lake covers 18,000 acres?

    J   A state park protects the Lake's wildlife.

Friday

5 **Read this sentence.**

Reelfoot Lake _____ by a series of earthquakes in 1811 and 1812.

Which word or words best complete this sentence?

    A   will form

    B   formed

    C   form

    D   was formed

Journal Writing Ideas

- Describe an activity that you enjoy or would like to try in a river, lake, pond, or ocean.

- Is it important to have parks and other nature preserves? Why?

Tennessee Geography

Monday

1 **Look at the underlined part of the sentence.**

The <u>Central Basin</u> is located in the middle of Tennessee.

Which answer shows the correct capitalization for the underlined part?

A central basin

B Central basin

C central Basin

D Correct as it is

Tuesday

2 **Read this sentence.**

_____ drew a colorful map of the state by ourselves.

Which words best complete this sentence?

F Tina and I

G Tina and me

H Me and Tina

J I and Tina

Wednesday

3 **Read the two sentences.**

Our state has plenty of rain. Our state has mild winters and useful soil.

What is the best way to combine these sentences?

A Our state has plenty of rain, and our state has mild winters and useful soil.

B Our state has plenty of rain and mild winters and useful soil.

C Our state has plenty of rain, mild winters, and useful soil.

D Our state has plenty of rain and mild winters, and our state has useful soil.

Tennessee Geography

Read the passage and look at the numbered, underlined parts. For Numbers 4 and 5, choose the answer that shows the correct capitalization and punctuation for each underlined part.

> My family is planning a trip to the Unaka <u>Mountains, Unaka</u> is the name of
> (4)
> an entire mountain range. "You can see <u>forever"! my</u> sister always says when we
> (5)
> hike there.

Thursday

4 F   mountains, Unaka

    G   Mountains. Unaka

    H   mountains. Unaka

    J   Correct as it is

Friday

5 A   forever!" my

    B   forever!" My

    C   forever?" My

    D   Correct as it is

Journal Writing Ideas

- Tennessee has mountains, farmland, rivers, and lakes. Describe the landscape in Tennessee that you like best.

- What do you like to do on a rainy day?

Tennessee Geography Week 24

Monday

1 **Which sentence is written correctly?**

A   Eastern Tennessee is in the appalachian mountains.

B   How does the land change as you travel westward.

C   Rolling hills and plains stretch west from the mountains.

D   "My homeland, Tennessee" is a song about the beauty of this land.

Tuesday

2 **Find the simple predicate, or action word, in the sentence.**

Trees <u>cover</u> more than <u>half</u> of the <u>land</u> in Tennessee.

F   G   H   J

Wednesday

3 **Find the sentence that is complete and written correctly.**

A   Riding horseback through Tennessee's woodlands.

B   To enjoy the wonderful sights, sounds, and smells.

C   You can rent horses at several of the state parks.

D   Guided horseback rides at Chickasaw State Park.

Tennessee Geography

For Numbers 4 and 5, choose the answer that shows the correct capitalization and punctuation to complete this information from a website.

Chickasaw State Park

20 Cabin Lane

_____ 38340

(4)

Horseback Riding

Horses can be rented from March though Thanksgiving weekend. Stables are open

_____.

(5)

Thursday

4 **F** Henderson, Tn   **H** Henderson TN

   G Henderson, TN   **J** Henderson, Tn

Friday

5 **A** Saturdays and sundays in the spring and fall

   B saturdays and sundays in the Spring and Fall

   C saturdays and Sundays in the Spring and Fall

   D Saturdays and Sundays in the spring and fall

Journal Writing Ideas

- If you had to choose between riding on a horse or riding in a car through Tennessee, which would you pick? Why?

- Describe some sights you have seen or might see while exploring in the woods.

Tennessee Tourist Attractions   Week 25

Monday

1   Which sentence is written correctly?

A   Did you ever go to Loretta Lynn's Ranch!

B   A model of her childhood Home in Butcher Holler Kentucky is there.

C   You can also see her Museum, the Coal Miners Daughter museum.

D   Her gold records, photos, and souvenirs of her career are on display.

Tuesday

2   Find the sentence that is complete and written correctly.

F   You can go to concerts there.

G   Also have fireworks sometimes.

H   My family camping in our tent.

J   Compete in a talent search?

Wednesday

3   Read this sentence.

We _____ Loretta Lynn herself in a great performance.

Which word or words best complete this sentence?

A   seen

B   saw

C   seeing

D   sees

© Houghton Mifflin Harcourt Publishing Company

Name _____

Tennessee Tourist Attractions

Week 25 (continued)

For Numbers 4 and 5, choose the answer that shows the correct capitalization and punctuation to complete the sign.

Welcome to Loretta Lynn's Ranch and Campground in _____
(4)

Join us for rail rides, camping, concerts, and fireworks. Fun for the entire

family! The season opens _____.
(5)

Thursday

4
- **F** Hurricane, Mills Tennessee
- **G** Hurricane Mills, Tennessee
- **H** Hurricane, Mills, Tennessee
- **J** Hurricane Mills Tennessee

Friday

5
- **A** April, 1 2006
- **B** April 1 2006
- **C** April 1, 2006
- **D** April, 1, 2006

Journal Writing Ideas

- Name some of your favorite tourist attractions. Describe one of them, using sensory words to make your description come alive.
- Describe your best summer vacation. What made it so special?

© Houghton Mifflin Harcourt Publishing Company

Tennessee Tourist Attractions   Week 26

Monday

1 **Which sentence is written correctly?**

A   Tennessee has so many wonderful museums?

B   The Museum of Appalachia is in Norris, Tennessee

C   It is like a real village in the Appalachian Mountains.

D   I liked the Quilts, the Toys, and the banjo music.

Tuesday

2 **Find the sentence that is complete and written correctly.**

F   A visit to the Memphis Rock and Soul Museum.

G   Learned about the history of rock and soul music.

H   This music began with country folks in the South.

J   Made instruments out of jugs, buckets, and washboards.

Wednesday

3 **Look at the underlined part of the sentence.**

"Have you been to the Tennessee <u>Aquarium" asked Destiny?</u>

Which answer shows the correct capitalization and punctuation for the underlined part?

A   Aquarium?" asked Destiny.

B   Aquarium," asked Destiny?

C   Aquarium"? asked Destiny.

D   Correct as it is

Tennessee Tourist Attractions

Week 26 (continued)

Read the passage and look at the numbered, underlined parts. For Numbers 4 and 5, choose the answer that shows the correct capitalization and punctuation for each underlined part.

The Tennessee Aquarium in Chattanooga takes you on a river journey you
                                                                    (4)
can visit a mountain forest where a river begins and see live songbirds, fish, and

otters, its also fun to experience the steamy river swamp with alligators and huge
  (5)
snapping turtles.

Thursday

4 **F** journey, you

G journey. You

H journey you

J Correct as it is

Friday

5 **A** otters, it's

B otters. Its

C otters. It's

D Correct as it is

Journal Writing Ideas

• Write about an experience you had at a science, history, or art museum.

• If you were to start a museum, what would you put in it?

Tennessee Tourist Attractions   Week 27

Monday

1 **Find the simple predicate, or action word, in the sentence.**

<u>We</u> <u>learned</u> <u>about</u> many <u>interesting</u> places in a vacation guide.

A   **B**   **C**   **D**

Tuesday

2 **Find the sentence that is complete and written correctly.**

F   We visited the Lookout Mountain Museum.

G   Rode the Incline Railway to the top of the mountain.

H   Seven states from the mountaintop!

J   Seemed to touch the clouds up there.

Wednesday

3 **Read this sentence.**

I believe that is the _____ place I have ever been.

Which word or words <u>best</u> complete this sentence?

A   most high

B   higher

C   more higher

D   highest

Tennessee Tourist Attractions

Read this paragraph. Then answer Numbers 4 and 5.

> ¹Rock City is on Lookout Mountain. ²Rock City is not a city at all. ³It is a mountainside trail filled with bridges, gardens, a waterfall and, of course, rocks. ⁴In the 1930s, ads for Rock City were painted on the sides of barns.

Thursday

4 **What is the best way to combine Sentences 1 and 2?**

F   Rock City is on Lookout Mountain, but Rock City is not a city at all.

G   Rock City is not a city at all, but it is on Lookout Mountain.

H   Rock City, on Lookout Mountain, is not a city at all.

J   Rock City is not a city on Lookout Mountain.

Friday

5 **What is the best way to write Sentence 4?**

A   In the 1930s, ads for Rock City was painted on the sides of barns.

B   In the 1930s, ads for Rock City are painted on the sides of barns.

C   In the 1930s, ads for Rock City is painted on the sides of barns.

D   Best as it is

Journal Writing Ideas

- Imagine that you just climbed a mountain. Describe your adventure.

- Write a poem about a mountain. Think of things you might see, hear, feel, and taste on a mountain.

Tennessee Tourist Attractions   Week 28

Monday

1 **Read this sentence.**

Have you ever _____ to Mud Island River Park?

Which word or words best complete this sentence?

A gone

B goed

C go

D went

Tuesday

2 **Which sentence is written correctly?**

F I went there with my family on my birthday?

G The park is in Memphis

H It's right on the Mississippi river.

J You can walk or take a monorail to the island.

Wednesday

3 **Find the simple subject, or naming word, in the sentence.**

My <u>family</u> <u>slept</u> in a tent on a <u>large</u> field <u>beside</u> the river.
      A **B**   **C**   **D**

Name _____

Tennessee Tourist Attractions   Week 28 (continued)

Thursday

4 **Look at the underlined part of the sentence.**

Everyone who was camping with us <u>said. "Happy</u> Birthday!"

Which answer shows the correct capitalization and punctuation for the underlined part?

F said, "happy

G Said. "happy

H said, "Happy

J Correct as it is

Friday

5 **Read the two sentences.**

You can rent a kayak at Mud Island River Park. You can take an airboat ride at Mud Island River Park.

What is the best way to combine these sentences?

A You can rent or take a kayak or an airboat ride at Mud Island River Park.

B You can rent a kayak at Mud Island River Park, or you can take an airboat ride at Mud Island River Park.

C You can rent a kayak or an airboat ride at Mud Island River Park.

D You can rent a kayak or take an airboat ride at Mud Island River Park.

Journal Writing Ideas

- What special thing did you once do on your birthday?
- Write about a day you spent on a river or a lake.

© Houghton Mifflin Harcourt Publishing Company

222 **WORKBOOK PLUS**
TCAP PRACTICE

Tennessee Government Week 29

Monday

1 **Find the simple predicate, or action word, in the sentence.**

In 1790, <u>Tennessee</u> <u>separated</u> <u>from</u> <u>North Carolina</u>.
　　　　　　A　　　　　B　　　　C　　　　D

Tuesday

2 **Find the sentence that is complete and written correctly.**

F　At that time, Tennessee became a territory.

G　William Blount the territorial governor.

H　Appointed governor by President Washington.

J　Blount strong and clever as governor.

Wednesday

3 **Which sentence is written correctly?**

A　Tennessee became a state in 1796.

B　It was the sixteenth state to join the United States?

C　Jonesboro, the oldest town, was founded in 1779

D　Knoxville was the first Capital of tennessee.

Tennessee Government

Read the passage and look at the numbered, underlined parts. For Numbers 4 and 5, choose the answer that shows the correct capitalization and punctuation for each underlined part.

> During the Civil War, Tennessee was the last Southern state to leave the
>
> <u>Union. And</u> the first to rejoin it. Tennessee was welcomed back into the United
>   **(4)**
> States on <u>july 24, 1866.</u>
>   **(5)**

Thursday

4 F Union. and

    G Union and

    H Union; And

    J Correct as it is

Friday

5 A July 24. 1866

    B July 24, 1866

    C July 24 1866

    D Correct as it is

Journal Writing Ideas

- What would you do if you were governor of the state of Tennessee?

- The frontier days were exciting. Describe some ways that life in Tennessee today is exciting.

Tennessee Government

Week 30

Monday

1 **Read the two sentences.**

In 1920, Harry Burn broke the tie on whether or not to let women vote. Burn was a Tennessee lawmaker.

What is the <u>best</u> way to combine these sentences?

A In 1920, Harry Burn broke the tie on whether or not to let women vote, and he was a Tennessee lawmaker.

B In 1920, Harry Burn was a Tennessee lawmaker, and Burn broke the tie on whether or not to let women vote.

C In 1920, Harry Burn, a Tennessee lawmaker, broke the tie on whether or not to let women vote.

D In 1920, Harry Burn broke the tie on whether or not to let women vote and was a Tennessee lawmaker.

Tuesday

2 **Look at the underlined part of the sentence.**

Harry Burn's mother believed in voting rights for <u>women, so</u> she told her son to support the new law.

Which answer shows the correct capitalization and punctuation for the underlined part?

F women So

G women. so

H women, So

J Correct as it is

© Houghton Mifflin Harcourt Publishing Company

Tennessee Government

Wednesday

3 **Read this sentence.**

Burn _____ his mother's advice on giving women the vote.

Which word or words best complete this sentence?

A take

B took

C taken

D had take

Thursday

4 **Find the sentence that is complete and correctly written.**

F Did not allow women to vote in some states.

G Needed thirty-six states in favor of the new law.

H Tennessee was the thirty-sixth state to pass it.

J The Nineteenth Amendment to the United States Constitution.

Friday

5 **Find the simple subject, or naming word, in the sentence below.**

Since 1920, American women have had the right to vote in every state.

A   B   C   D

Journal Writing Ideas

- Why do you think it is important to vote in a national election?

- Would you like to run for a public office? Explain your answer.

© Houghton Mifflin Harcourt Publishing Company

Name _____

Tennessee Government   **Week 31**

Monday

1 **Find the adjective, or describing word, in the sentence.**

Andrew <u>Johnson</u> <u>opened</u> a <u>small</u> tailor shop in <u>Greeneville</u>.
        A   **B**   **C**   **D**

Tuesday

2 **Find the sentence that is complete and written correctly.**

F Andrew Johnson with less education than any other president.

G Learned to read when seventeen years old.

H Johnson was a tailor before becoming a lawmaker.

J Held many public offices and was governor of Tennessee.

Wednesday

3 **Read this sentence.**

Johnson _____ the office of president when President Abraham Lincoln was killed in office.

Which word or words best complete this sentence?

A fill

B will fill

C filled

D filling

Tennessee Government

For Numbers 4 and 5, choose the answer that shows the correct capitalization and punctuation to complete the sign.

Andrew Johnson National Historic Site

_____ 37744
(4)

Johnson served as the seventeenth president of the United States from

_____.
(5)

Thursday

4 **F** Greeneville, Tennessee   **H** greeneville, tennessee

   G Greeneville, tennessee   **J** greeneville, Tennessee

Friday

5 **A** April 15, 1865, to March 3, 1869

   B April, 15 1865, to March, 3 1869

   C April 15 1865 to March 3 1869

   D April, 15, 1865, to March, 3, 1869

Journal Writing Ideas

• What are some personal qualities that are important for a president to have?

• Who do you think was the best president of the United States? Explain.

Tennessee Government

Week 32

Monday

1 **Look at the underlined part of the sentence.**

Miss LeRoy <u>said "the</u> three branches of Tennessee's government do three different jobs."

Which answer shows the correct capitalization and punctuation for the underlined part?

A said "The

B said, "the

C said, "The

D Correct as it is

Tuesday

2 **Read this sentence.**

In Tennessee, new laws _____ created by the legislative branch of the government.

Which word or words best complete this sentence?

F are

G has been

H is

J be

Wednesday

3 **Find the answer that is complete and written correctly.**

A The executive branch of the Tennessee government.

B Responsible for making sure the laws are obeyed.

C Also runs the day-to-day business of the government.

D The head of the executive branch is the governor.

Tennessee Government

Read this paragraph. Then answer Numbers 4 and 5.

> [1]Yesterday we learn about the judicial system. [2]When citizens are accused of breaking the law, court judges can settle the matter. [3]Judges listen to both sides. [4]They ask questions. [5]They come to a decision.

Thursday

4 **What is the <u>best</u> way to write Sentence 1?**

    F   Yesterday we learning about the judicial system.

    G   Yesterday we was learning about the judicial system.

    H   Yesterday we learned about the judicial system.

    J   Correct as it is

Friday

5 **What is the <u>best</u> way to combine Sentences 3, 4, and 5?**

    A   Judges listen to both sides, and they ask questions, and they come to a decision.

    B   Judges listen to both sides, ask questions, and come to a decision.

    C   Judges listen to both sides and ask questions, or they come to a decision.

    D   Judges listen to both sides ask questions, and they come to a decision.

Journal Writing Ideas

- What do you think it means to be a fair judge?

- Why do you think a government sometimes needs to create new laws?

Tennessee Trivia

Monday

1 **Find the simple predicate, or action word, in the sentence.**

General Daniel Smith named the state of Tennessee.
   A   **B**   **C**   **D**

Tuesday

2 **Find the sentence that is complete and written correctly.**

F   Alex Haley, famous writer of the book *Roots*.

G   Haley came from Henning, Tennessee.

H   Trace several generations in Haley's family.

J   A Pulitzer Prize for the book!

Wednesday

3 **Look at the underlined part of the sentence.**

Barry asked. "Did you ever visit the Car Collector's Hall of Fame in Nashville?"

Which answer shows the correct capitalization and punctuation of the underlined part?

A   asked, "did

B   asked? "Did

C   asked, "Did

D   Correct as it is

Tennessee Trivia

Thursday

4 **Read the two sentences.**

A county in Tennessee is named after Davy Crockett. He was a famous woodsman.

What is the <u>best</u> way to combine these sentences?

F A county in Tennessee is named after Davy Crockett, a famous woodsman.

G A famous woodsman named a county in Tennessee after Davy Crockett.

H A famous county in Tennessee is named after Davy Crockett, a woodsman.

J A county in Tennessee is named after Davy Crockett, and he was a famous woodsman.

Friday

5 **Which sentence is written correctly?**

A Glen Millers band made "Chattanooga Choo Choo" a famous song.

B Glen millers band made "Chattanooga Choo Choo" a famous song.

C Glen miller's band made "Chattanooga Choo Choo" a famous song.

D Glen Miller's band made "Chattanooga Choo Choo" a famous song.

Journal Writing Ideas

- Do you like to play trivia games? Why or why not?

- The book *Roots* is about finding one's ancestors. Write about your own ancestors.

Tennessee Trivia

Monday

1 **Find the adjective, or describing word, in the sentence.**

Cordell <u>Hull</u> <u>was</u> a <u>great</u> leader from <u>Tennessee</u>.

    A **B**   **C**   **D**

Tuesday

2 **Which sentence is written correctly?**

F   In 1867, John muir hiked 1000 miles to the Gulf of Mexico.

G   Muir crossed the Cumberland Mountains on his way through Tennessee?

H   Workers had cut a Tunnel through Cumberland mountain in 1849.

J   Imagine doing that work, using mostly picks and shovels!

Wednesday

3 **Find the sentence that is complete and written correctly.**

A   June Carter Cash and Johnny Cash lived in Tennessee for many years.

B   Their home known as the House of Cash.

C   For a while, a museum.

D   Located in Hendersonville, Tennessee.

Tennessee Trivia

For Numbers 4 and 5, choose the answer that uses the correct capitalization and punctuation to complete the sign.

> Welcome to _____, Home of the Manhattan Project. Atomic
> (4)
> weapons made here were first used on _____.
> (5)
> Many believe that their use helped to bring an end to World War II.

Thursday

4 **F** Oak ridge, Tennessee   **H** oak Ridge, Tennessee

     G Oak Ridge, tennessee   **J** Oak Ridge, Tennessee

Friday

5 **A** August, 6, 1945   **C** August, 6 1945

     B August 6, 1945   **D** August 6 1945

Journal Writing Ideas

- Pretend that you are a movie producer who wants to film a movie set in Tennessee. Write about your plans for this movie. Where will it be filmed? Who will act in it? What will the movie be about?

- Do you know any trivia about Tennessee? Write about it for your classmates.

© Houghton Mifflin Harcourt Publishing Company

Tennessee Trivia

Monday

1 **Read this sentence.**

Bessie Smith, one of the _____ of all blues singers, was born in Chattanooga.

Which word or words best complete this sentence?

A most greatest

C most great

B great

D greatest

Tuesday

2 **Look at the underlined part of the sentence.**

"What Tennessee basketball coach wrote the book *Reach for the Summit"* asked Erin?

Which answer shows the correct punctuation for the underlined part?

F *Summit,"* asked Erin?

H *Summit"*? asked Erin.

G *Summit?"* asked Erin.

J Correct as it is

Wednesday

3 **Read the two sentences.**

Tennessee runner Wilma Rudolph was a great athlete. Wilma Rudolph won three Olympic gold medals.

What is the best way to combine these sentences?

A Tennessee runner Wilma Rudolph was a great athlete, and Wilma Rudolph won three Olympic gold medals.

B Tennessee runner Wilma Rudolph was a great athlete and won three Olympic gold medals.

C Tennessee runner Wilma Rudolph was a great athlete, so Wilma Rudolph won three Olympic gold medals.

D Tennessee runner Wilma Rudolph was a great athlete, or she won three Olympic gold medals.

Tennessee Trivia

Read the passage and look at the numbered, underlined parts. For Numbers 4 and 5, choose the answer that shows the correct capitalization and punctuation for each underlined part.

> Robert Church, Sr., started life as a <u>slave but</u> he became the first
> (4)
> African-American millionaire in the South. Church lived in Memphis after the
> Civil War and developed many successful <u>businesses. He</u> also created an
> (5)
> important arts and culture center for the African-American community.

Thursday

4
- **F** slave, but
- **G** slave But
- **H** slave. But
- **J** Best as it is

Friday

5
- **A** businesses, he
- **B** businesses he
- **C** businesses and he
- **D** Best as it is

Journal Writing Ideas

- What person or place in your community might become famous in the future? Why do you think so?
- What advice would you give people who want to achieve their dreams?

Tennessee Trivia   Week 36

Monday

1 **Find the simple subject, or naming word, in the sentence.**

Our <u>class</u> <u>visited</u> the Jonesborough <u>History</u> Museum.
A B C   D

Tuesday

2 **Find the sentence that is complete and written correctly.**

F   Sam Davis's home still on Sam Davis Road in Smyrna.

G   Davis a hero of the Confederacy.

H   He was captured by Union troops.

J   Statue of Davis on the grounds of the Tennessee Capitol.

Wednesday

3 **Which sentence is written correctly?**

A   The carnton Mansion was built in 1826.

B   Is it the oldest building in Franklin?

C   the house was used as a hospital during the Battle of Franklin

D   Were the patients Union or Confederate soldiers.

Tennessee Trivia

Read this paragraph. Then answer Numbers 4 and 5.

> [1]Patricia McKissack and Frederick McKissack often write books together. [2]Frederick McKissack is Patricia's husband. [3]Many of their books tell the stories of various African Americans. [4]When she is a child, Patricia spent many hours in the library. [5]It was one of the few places in Nashville that was not segregated.

Thursday

4 **What is the best way to combine Sentences 1 and 2?**

F Patricia McKissack's husband, Frederick, often write books together.

G Patricia McKissack and her husband, Frederick McKissack, often write books together.

H Patricia McKissack and Frederick McKissack often write books together because Frederick McKissack is Patricia's husband.

J Patricia McKissack and Frederick McKissack often write books together with Patricia's husband.

Friday

5 **What is the best way to write Sentence 4?**

A When she is a child, Patricia will spend many hours in the library.

B When she was a child, Patricia spends many hours in the library.

C When she was a child, Patricia spent many hours in the library.

D Best as it is

Journal Writing Ideas

- Write about a museum or other building that you have visited.

- Would you like to be an author? What would you write about?